More
THAN A MUM

Copyright © 2018
All rights reserved. This book or any portion thereof may not be reproduced or used in any manner whatsoever without the express written permission of the author except for the use of brief quotations in a book review.
Printed in Australia
First Printing, 2018
ISBN: 978-0-6482128-3-6
White Light Publishing House
Melton, VIC, Australia 3337

whitelightpublishing.com.au

Foreword

Motherhood is possibly the most important thing that will ever happen to a woman in her life. It affects everything - how you feel, how you live, how you see the world and, in many ways, both good and bad, it turns your life upside down.

For me, motherhood meant I no longer knew who I was. The old me was gone and the new me, well, she was here but who was she? What was my purpose, was I destined to fold washing and rock and pat for the rest of my life? Or was I supposed to continue on in my old life and go back to work? And yet, how could I go back to work? How could I leave this precious being that even though was no longer inside still felt like part of me?

This is the dilemma faced by millions of women all over the world. The decision to be a stay at home mum or be a working mum is not something that women take lightly. But, what if there was another way? A way that she could fulfil her potential and make an income while still being fully involved in her baby's life?

What if she could actually 'have it all'?

Becoming a mumpreneur has been the most rewarding experience for me, allowing me to have freedom, flexibility, family time and financial independence. I've defined success on my own terms and discovered new talents, strengths and a courage I'd never known existed before. Since embarking on the journey to become 'more than a mum' I've worked with thousands of women, including many of the women you'll meet in this book.

I believe that right now a new version of feminism is emerging – and mumpreneurs are driving this movement. Mothering is important; it's crucial to the survival of the human race. Yet, with all the best intentions, the original feminist movement didn't get it quite right, especially for mothers. For the last forty years, women have tried to 'fit in' to a system that was never designed with them in mind. The 9-5 was designed by men, for men. This was never the way women would have set things up if they'd been in charge from the start.

The mumpreneur movement is a reflection of women now creating a system and a lifestyle that works for them, with more consideration for flexibility, family time, productivity and financial independence. It's the evolution of feminism; women standing up and saying, "You know what? The old way of working doesn't work for me, so I'm going to forge my own path."

Mumpreneurs are fast paced, productive and smart. They can work from anywhere and they make their business work for them. Often, they're highly experienced and educated women with successful corporate careers behind them who find that once they become a mother, their whole world changes and they want to find a new way to be this new person that allows them to embrace both career and motherhood.

The recent surge of women becoming mumpreneurs is not a coincidence.

It's women standing up and saying: "We're not going to put up with the old ways of doing things anymore. We're going out on our own and we're going to create something new, so that we can work on our own terms and create a life that works for us and for our families."

This book explores the experiences of courageous women who have done just that and dared to take the path of an entrepreneur while balancing motherhood too.

Peace Mitchell

Peace Mitchell is the co-founder of AusMumpreneur, Australia's #1 community for mums in business, and the Women's Business School, which provides flexible and time efficient business education for women who've started their own business.

www.ausmumpreneur.com
www.thewomensbusinessschool.com

Always go with the choice that scares you the most, because that's the one that is going to require the most from you. Do you really want to look back on your life and see how wonderful it could have been had you not been afraid to live it?

-Caroline Myss

Introduction

In recent years, I have been blessed enough to connect with so many amazing women who are not only spectacular Mummas but are also running their own businesses, and that is how the idea for this book came about. I wanted to create a collection of stories from real women to help inspire and encourage other Mums out there to follow their true passions, and to see for themselves that having it all *is* possible.

When I was nominated for an AusMumpreneur award in 2016, I was quite hesitant about attending the conference and awards. To be honest, I was expecting was a room full of corporate, stuck-up women who wouldn't be interested in associating with someone like me who ran a small business from home and wasn't even drawing an income yet. Instead, what I found was a tribe of women I never knew existed. Every single Mumma there was in fact, just like me – in the most important way. Passionate about what they did in their business and wanting to make a difference in the world, in one way or another. These women were some of the most empowering, inspirational souls I had ever met, and the entire experience was all about celebrating our greatness - as both Mums and business owners – and helping to raise one another up.

Needless to say, the weekend was ah-mazing! I now attend every year and have made some beautiful long-lasting connections with some of those Mummas, some of which are featured here in this very book. If you've never heard of the AusMumpreneur network, do yourself a favour and connect with this brilliant tribe of powerful women. I cannot speak highly enough of them.

Of course, amazing women like this can be found everywhere. The Mums featured in this book are from all around the world. Some are still in the early phases of their business, some have been doing it for years. Regardless of whether you are an experienced and long-term business owner, are just starting up, or are even still in the stages of wondering whether to go down that road, you will find these stories inspiring and full of wisdom. If you're anything like me, you'll likely have a mixture of emotions while reading these women's stories, as you find just how familiar their experiences are to your own.

I want to say a massive thank you to all of the spectacular Mummas who contributed to this book. You are all amazing, and I am honoured that you have shared your very personal journeys with us here for the world to read. May your lives always be filled with joy and abundance of every kind.

Much love,

Everyone has been made for some particular work, and the desire for that work has been put in every heart.
–**Rumi**

Contents

Ali Knights	15
Ashley Brown	29
Bronte Spicer	45
Ellen Lorraine Niemeier	61
Hayley Scott	79
Jennifer Forest	97
Joanne Giles	103
Kelly McDonald	113
Natalee Anderson	123
Rochelle Muscat	139
Samantha Young	157
Susanna Heiskanen	171
Talita Sheedy	181
Tracey Farrelly	191
Ruchika Rawat	201
Laura McNally	207
Anu Sawhney	221
Claire Orange	231
Emma Lovell	247
Jessica McCarroll	253
Karen Koutsodontis	261
Katharine Rattray	267
Melissa Woodward	283
Karen McDermott	299
Christie Lyons	309
More about our Authors	319

Ali Knights

KIN balance

Ali Knights is a mother of two and a founder of KIN balance, a natural therapy supporting families and individuals. Launching her business in 2015, she has had two onsite school clinics in remote South Australia and supports families all over Australia.

But, who am I? Who am I to be chosen to share my story? I am a mum, a wife, and a small business owner living in a small mining town in outback South Australia. I have often asked myself that question over the past few years, plagued with doubt and feeling like a fraud. Who am I to be doing this? Sound familiar? My greatest learning since launching my business has been to proudly shine a light on myself, stand tall and recognise that I am (you are) … well, amazing.

So, who am I? I am the mother of two completely divine young men, Jarvis (6) and Fraser (4). Their love is intoxicating and all consuming, and their energy is never ending! I am the wife to a man who I fell in love with when I was seventeen and have been lucky enough to be married to for the last ten years. I am also a mum to three angel babies who have blessed me with their very short presence and everlasting love. I am a school teacher, an empath, a daughter, a sister and a friend to some absolute legends. I am also the person that puts on her pyjamas the second I walk through the door and knows that chocolate is for every occasion. All of these hats bring with them their own lessons, learnings and blessings. Instead of down-playing or undervaluing these different aspects of my life, I have learnt to embrace them and see them as the things that set me apart from everyone else in the business world.

I have learnt that being anyone but myself is just a waste.

Do I have it all figured out yet? No. Have I overcome all of my self-doubt and sabotage? No chance. But, I have made mighty big inroads and I hope that by sharing my story I can give you a few shortcuts along your business journey. My story started with a mighty big hiccup. My life got turned upside down and I clung to my sanity by studying. Now there is no turning back, so I am just enjoying the ride.

Finding my calm in the chaos. In early 2015 the big C came crashing into our lives, head first without warning. My very fit and health hubby one day had a sore shoulder and a few agonizing weeks later, he was diagnosed with Non-Hodgkin's Lymphoma. My youngest, Fraser, was only eighteen months old and Jarvis had just started kindergarten. Within a month of diagnosis, his spleen was removed, and we were travelling 650kms to his chemo lounge every fortnight. Panic, anxiety and overwhelming feelings struck my family.

A few months before this, I had signed up to study a natural therapy called The Zoi Method, which was due to start a few weeks after diagnosis. When I called to quit the course, my teacher told me this was even more reason to study, to learn, to support. So, as I clung to my family and sanity, I began my study.

During the day-long chemo sessions, Wes would listen to music and try to sleep the ordeal away and I would sit beside him with my books and study. He became my study partner and test subject. In the days after his chemo, he would crash with nausea, vomiting and so physically exhausted that he would just lay in bed or sit for long periods of time on the shower floor. I would sit next to the bed and flush his meridians or balance his energy and then within an hour, he would be up playing with the boys. Each time it would buy him hours of crucial bonding time and bring some normality back in our lives. This is when I knew I was onto a good thing! We were living, breathing, daily testaments to how powerful this gorgeous modality was.

For the next year, I drove, sat, played, laughed, cried, worked and studied. We decided that we would make this time count, leaving all regrets at the door. It wasn't easy and often I would wake at 2am silently sobbing while lying next to the love of my life who was fighting with every part of his being to be healthy again. But, we made it!

A year after his initial diagnosis, Wes was in remission and I was officially finishing my first round of study. I knew without any doubt that the mix of eastern and western medicine got us through. The chemo killed the cancer and the energy healing kept his body strong enough to keep fighting and healing. It's all about balance.

Weeks after, we settled back into home life again and I opened the doors to my clinic. We haven't looked back.

KIN balance – My balance. Since 2015, I have become accredited in two more energy healing modalities and I now blend them all together in a little sacred bubble and business I call KIN balance. I am a Holistic Energy Practitioner. I support people in reducing anxiety, getting a full night's sleep and connecting to their true selves. I balance the body, mind and soul from newborns to the elderly ... and I absolutely love it!

I work with people face-to-face in my town of Roxby Downs and I have clients all over Australia who I support with remote balances. That is the amazing thing about energy. There are no boundaries and so many benefits. A large number of my clients are my little kindred souls - babies and children who need support with sleep, attachment, or to calm their anxiety. I educate children on how emotions affect their bodies and how to recognise and move through different emotions.

In 2016, I won a grant to have an onsite clinic at our local high school, supporting teens at risk and next month, I launch at a new school in a neighbouring town. The focus for these students is clearing any past or present emotional blocks in their body that causes them to have low self-esteem, panic attacks, anger issues or to detach from their learning. I also work with students with autism or heightened sensory needs; focusing on reducing anxiety, improving sleep and understanding how their emotions can affect their body and behaviour.

I am so passionate about empowering our youth to embrace their individuality and proudly shine light on all of their skills and talents. How amazing is it that I get to do this in such a unique, gentle, yet powerful way? As a teacher by profession, I love being able to support students on a whole new level.

It has been only two years since I officially opened my door and I am loving this ride!

Guilt vs Content. Since the launch of KIN balance, life has been hectic with a small side of calm. When I step into my practitioner's room, a peace comes over me and I just float around my clients. I feel a mixture of calm and content - an inner knowing that this is where I need to be. I have absolutely found something I love to do, but sometimes getting to the room is anything but calm. Guilt is the strongest emotion that took over my first year, and still creeps in. Guilt for spending so much time and energy away from my family. Guilt for missing out on so much with them. Guilt for spending so much time and energy on others. Often, the last sounds I would hear as I walked out the front door was one of the boys crying and the other asking, "why are you going to work *again* mum?" Kids know how to put just the right amount of pressure on to make your heart ache. It took me some time to realise they were only feeding off my emotions.

It took a lot to get my head around the fact that my business was a 'real job' and not just a hobby. I would happily put the boys in daycare or after-hours school care for the couple of days I still taught at the school but would be wracked with guilt at the thought of doing this for my own business. I needed a whole change of mindset. I needed to remember that the quality of time I had with my friends and family was important, not the quantity of it. It's that simple.

If putting them in care or not being there for two nights a week to tuck them in meant that I could be totally present, phone away when I was with them, then that was worth it. I also found putting a bit of my KIN balance money away each week to go towards a weekend trip as a family gave me something to look forward to on the days I struggled with guilt. And to be honest, I am a better and happier person after I balance. It leaves me with a glow and calm that I hadn't experienced before. Doing what I do makes me a happier, calmer person, which ultimately helps everyone.

After guilt, the second most powerful emotion I am still working through is self-doubt. I remembered reading all these blogs, quotes and hearing all these stories about 'when you find your passion it doesn't feel like work at all'. Often, I do feel like this because I love what I do and am energised at the thought of my day. But, I also still have my days where I struggle to get motivated or feel like I am dragging myself to the room. On these days, I am left wondering how, if I love what I am doing and it's my soul's calling, why aren't I doing my happy dance every day?

My realisation ... it's still work!

This isn't a negative, just a reality. I do love what I do. I love how much I am learning and making a difference. But, I still need to stay up late to get things done. I still need early morning starts to feel on top of everything. I am still tired some days and just want to stay home on the couch and watch a movie (or two).

To make it work, I need to work. The good news is now I get to make it work on my own terms. To pick the work hours that work for me and my family. To wear what I want to wear, communicate how I choose and be inspired to grow and change organically. It's freedom of a whole new sort.

Let this be a lesson that I learnt for you, so you don't have to ... leave the self-doubt behind. You don't need to love every second of what you do. Give yourself permission to feel tired and unmotivated sometimes, to feel like it is all too hard and one big mistake. That is life; that is growth. Tomorrow you will see it all with fresh eyes and you will be motivated and in the flow. Life is all about balance and your outlook on your business needs to be, too.

My hot tip ... Find time for you. There are lots of late nights in front of the computer, especially in the start-up phase. It is easy to get consumed with your 'to do' list, but important to keep the balance in your life.

Starting a new business doesn't mean stopping everything else.

Hobbies are even more important now. Make sure you keep time for the things that you love and bring you some peace or stop that mental chatter. For me, this is sports. I can be active, social and I am forced to concentrate solely on something else all at once. What is it that brings you this release?

Find your village. They say it takes a village to raise a child. Well, it takes another to have your own business. You cannot go at this alone and really, why would you want to? You are surrounded by so many people with different skill sets, opinions and expertise, so why not make the most of it?

Initially I thought starting my own business would be quite isolating, especially coming from an education background where I constantly worked collaboratively with other teachers. I went into this with the same headset.

Who can I learn from? I realised that I had surrounded myself with friends with so many different skill-sets and that there are many different ways to seek support. They might not have in-depth knowledge in natural health modalities, but they have helped in so many other ways. Entrepreneurial friends or those with a business headset have offered me advice, collaborated, edited my work or put me onto courses or books that have been invaluable to them. Informally (and sometimes, more importantly) just having people around to run my ideas past, listen with an open ear, drop dinner around when things are crazy, have the boys for play dates or drink wine with me when I need to get out of my head has been priceless to me. They have been amazing.

I am now starting to build up a bit of an online village whom I can learn from and gain support from in different ways. I have joined some fantastic female business Facebook forums and pages that I highly recommend to anyone starting out.

This year, I have put money back into the business and my growth within it. I started monthly sessions with a business coach who keeps me in balance and accountable for my own growth. I have enrolled in a business course which has enabled me to gain knowledge, plus also connect with other women around Australia who are in the foundation stages of their businesses, too. I am also currently on the look-out to hire someone who can update and revamp my website.

Let's not forget the most important people in your village, your family. Wes has been my number one supporter for which I am eternally grateful. My parents are wonderful sounding boards and so supportive with my kids when we visit Adelaide or come up here, so I can attend further study. As you can see, my village is large and vast. Currently my business is only small, but I know that as it grows it is crucial to keep adding people in who are going to add depth and knowledge to my vision.

Raw and Real. While I am very passionate about what I do, it doesn't mean the process has been smooth. At times, it has been anything but. There have been many hurdles over the past couple of years and no doubt there'll many ahead. So, from one soul Mumma to another, here are my biggest learnings:

Be present.
There are so many hats to juggle. I learnt the hard way that I needed to get organised and plan my time better. Initially, I was so focused on building my business, that when a new client wanted an appointment I would work around them. WRONG! After wearing myself out and missing out on so many play dates with my boys, I started to resent the work I was doing because it felt hard and draining. I had this picture in my head that this flexible lifestyle would allow for more time with my family, but I felt I was missing out on so much more.

My hubby finally had to have a hard word with me. Wes could see I was drowning. He told me I needed to stop putting everyone first and start setting boundaries. As a born 'people pleaser' this did not sit well with me [insert tears and frustration], but I knew he was right. I learnt to be firm with my work hours and put down the phone. This allowed me to be present with my family, my friends and my work.

I learnt that each time I said 'no' to others, I was saying 'yes' to myself and my family.

People will wait for a response.
People will come to you during your set hours. They do it for every other business, so why not yours? There will always be an adjustment period when you first start to work out which hours or days work best for both you and your clients. Allow this wiggle room, then give yourself permission to be firm with them. You do not need to be on call 24 hours a day. If you respect and value your time, others will too.

Know your target audience.
Living in a small mining town, my biggest obstacle was 'making the alternative mainstream'. I know that natural therapies are not for everyone, but I also know how much benefit you can gain from them. I needed to be smart about how I spread my message.

I focused on getting results from those who I knew needed it most in my town ... mums. My town is very unique as the average age of the population is in the late twenties. For many years, we had the highest birth-rate per capita in Australia. Young couples move to town to get ahead and set themselves up, then they start their families. These women are part of mothers' groups and have large social circles. Therefore, it made sense that this was my initial target audience.

Once word spread about how I could connect babies back to sleep, or balance women's hormones after birth in a non-invasive way, people wanted to know more. By connecting with this target group early, it allowed me to grow quickly.

Who is *your* target audience? Not just male or female, but what age, relationship status, hobbies, favourite types of social media and so on? Really dig deep into what your ideal customer or client is like, because it will give you so much more clarity into how and where you advertise and market yourself.

Get really clear in order to get great results.

While this was my initial target audience, I now see a broad range of people as word spread about my service. The number of male clients coming through the doors are growing each month and now, my key demographic is teenagers. I love how I get to support the whole family.

Charge your worth.
Your time is money! Each minute you are spending in your business, with a client or customer, is time you are not spending with your kids or loved ones. It is okay to charge accordingly for this.

Initially, I would charge enough to cover materials and day-care. If a friend was watching the boys, then I would have even more trouble charging because 'it wasn't costing me anything to be here'. But, when I am with a client, I am not with my boys. I am not relaxing on the couch with my husband or hanging out with friends and family. I need to charge accordingly for this because my time is precious and so is yours!

Do you know what else is precious? Your unique skills, ability, wisdom and knowledge. No one else has the perfect mix of you, but you. This needs to be considered in your pricing, too.

You are worthy of success.
This was a big one for me. I have three university degrees: Education, Disability Studies and an Arts degree. I have coached national teams in the Special Olympics and taught students in a school setting from reception to Year 11. But, I did not go to university for four years to study natural therapies, so how can I call myself a professional at what I now do? Who am I to do this work? I am not gifted, special, nor do I meditate daily or live by the moon cycles. I have moments where I feel like a fraud. But, then I remember that I am not putting myself out there as all these things.

I am not trying to be something I am not, *and* I am helping people. I am sharing my learning and making people happier, healthier and more connected. I am helping other mums, partners and children just like my own. I am supporting women who have felt the same heartache and loss as I have move through this grief.

**That is why I am good at what I do ...
because I am me.**

Whatever your business is or is going to be, you are the perfect person for it. Your life experience, passion, learnings, goals, connections, heartbreaks and greatest joys are what is going to make you a success. All of it! Your skill set is so much broader than you give yourself credit for.

To infinity and beyond. Initially, I started studying so I could help my family stay happy and healthy. My eldest child can get quite anxious, so I knew this would be a great way to support him to grow. As I learnt more, I wanted to share it with others. I brainstormed and registered a name, created a temporary logo using an app, started a Facebook page and just put it out there.

Like I said earlier, now I am just enjoying the ride. Everything has happened so quickly, but at the same time I feel like I have been doing this forever. I absolutely love supporting people to reconnect to health and happiness and wouldn't change a thing about the last couple of years.

Moving forward, I plan to expand into new schools and educational settings, setting up clinics and teaching simple energy hygiene and self-regulation skills to children of all ages and abilities. If we can reduce the anxiety, we can improve the learning and growth opportunities. This results in deeper connections, stronger friendships and improved self-worth. I help babies sleep, depression to lift, confidence build, and support women's transition into motherhood. What isn't there to love?

So, what are you waiting for? If your intention is pure, your ideas driven by passion and you honour your skills and abilities, then nothing can stop you from creating magic. Give yourself permission to jump. Your village will catch you.

Ashley Brown

Sosocii Pty Ltd

Over the years I've continually refined my ability to adapt to new situations. Just when I began to feel comfortable and settled, something was on its way to shake all that up and keep me on my feet. Experiencing these seemingly endless adjustments, saw me develop a resilience which has been extremely beneficial throughout my journey of ups and downs in my personal life and within my business endeavours. Developing my capacity to endure unexpected emotional challenges whilst continuing to push myself towards my goals. Fostering my personal strengths and acknowledging my ability to survive and even thrive. Finally finding my inner self-confidence, embracing a sense of gratitude for all the positives and remembering to have faith in my own unique journey.

> In order to love who you are, you cannot hate the experiences that shaped you.
> Andrea Dykstra

As a young child, I grew up in very remote rural areas throughout New South Wales and Queensland. My father managed farms whilst my mother wrangled three girls under five. It was the epitome of free-range childhoods; climbing trees, building forts, mustering cattle on horseback, riding motorbikes and even driving cars several kilometers to the bus stop. We cuddled the baby animals, grew up on the fresh unpasteurized milk, caught yabbies in the dam and went camping by the river. We were also aware of the harsh bush realities, like watching animals go from paddock to dinner plate, dust storms flying through the verandas and seeing bushfires on the horizon.

Every few years, my father seemed to crave a fresh start and hence we'd pack up all of our belongings and move to a new house again – a routine we became accustomed to and began to anticipate - constantly transitioning from one location to the next; from rolling green hills to incredibly remote and desolate red dirt areas ravaged by severe droughts. A life without radio and television signals seemingly explains my lack of the pop culture references my peers possess. Of course, these moves forced a change of schools and so I became an expert at making new friends, refining my networking skills from a young age. However, it was my two best friends, my younger sisters who indulged my bossy big sister persona and lovingly subjected themselves to hours on the veranda playing schools. It was this marvelous pretend play that most likely planted the seed that later saw me study a Bachelor of Education.

Tapping into my juvenile intuition, I seemingly sensed my parents' impending separation. I began to dream about it, perhaps subtly preparing myself for what soon became my reality. After spending time with both parents in their new lives as solo parents, I began my first rollercoaster of seemingly difficult emotions, which ultimately saw me opting to relocate to live with my mother in the centre of Melbourne. This was such a dramatic leap, as the city was such a stark contrast to the rural lifestyle I had become accustomed to. The schooling transition was where I experienced the biggest shock and it took quite some time to settle into what seemed a completely different culture.

> **You don't have a right to the cards you believe you should have been dealt. You have an obligation to play the hell out of the ones you're holding.**
> Cheryl Strayed

My mother was such a huge inspiration to me throughout my teenage years. I watched her raise three teenage daughters whilst juggling full time work, studying and paying off a mortgage. She had so little time for herself, and yet she managed to channel all of her energy into creating a comfortable life for us all. Being raised by such a strong woman put me in good stead for having to overcome my own life juggles and to find the strength to get me through times of hardship.

In the later years of high school, I was torn between studying marketing, teaching or nursing at university. I decided to study a Bachelor of Education. Having plenty of experience with children through babysitting and possessing a nurturing personality, it seemed like the ideal fit for me. I couldn't really imagine doing anything else and I am a big believer in trusting your gut instincts. So, in a massive leap of independence, I moved an hour and a half from my family to attend university in Ballarat.

I enjoyed the new-found freedom and fun of the university lifestyle - renting my own house and setting up for the big transition into independent adult life. I was lucky enough to travel to Europe at eighteen, finding myself in awe as I had such amazing experiences exploring other cultures. Then, I quickly found myself engaged to my boyfriend and consequently began to settle down, buying a house and embracing the security of domestic stability in my early twenties. I worked as an after-school care assistant and vacation care leader whist studying to become a teacher. But, it was my work as a research assistant at the university that gave me the contrast I craved.

You get in life, what you have the courage to ask for.
Oprah Winfrey

After completing my Bachelor of Education, I was delighted to secure a teaching position at a beautiful rural school not all that far away. I happily taught grades in the prep-2 area for almost five years. I relocated once again, before marrying at the age of twenty-four. I continued to travel internationally and had really picked up the desire to tick so many countries off that ever-growing list of locations I must see before I die. However, it was the moment I realised I was pregnant with my first child that I suddenly felt a sense of being complete. I had been craving the stage of motherhood for as long as I could remember. Despite the intense morning sickness, I was in a state of euphoria anticipating the arrival of my own bundle of joy. Overcoming a traumatic labour and the subsequent road to recovery didn't dampen my state of bliss as I cradled my precious daughter. Life had become oh so much richer following her arrival.

I'll never forget those tiny hands wrapped around my fingers. Her cheeky smiles and squeals of laughter. Watching her sleep, grow, learn to walk and talk. Discovering her enthusiasm for books, painting, music and dancing. I will not forget the constant stress over whether she was eating enough, the midnight fevers, the sleepless nights and the massive tantrums. Nonetheless, she had become my world, my reason for living, the love of my life.

> **Life is not measured by the number of breaths we take, but by the moments that take our breath away.**
> Maya Angelou

As I watched her grow, I lamented the thought of returning to full time teaching. I longed for increased flexibility to watch her grow and make those special memories, whilst maintaining my career ambitions as well. So, I began to consider my skill set and my interests. Deciding on several avenues I could pursue and discussing them with friends and family, I researched the steps involved in each business venture and weighed up the overall flexibility they would provide. Ultimately, I wanted the work to be predominantly online so that I could work in the evening hours when my baby was asleep. So, I slowly developed my experience in online administration and social media marketing through my sister's bridal couture business. Once I had established my confidence and honed my skills, I then went out on my own and created Sosocii Pty Ltd.

I launched Sosocii Pty Ltd in December 2014 - initially providing social media management and then later, expanding services to include virtual administrative support. 'Socii' is Latin for allies and so I built the name around this word, creating 'Sosocii' as a unique brand. I wanted to build the business around the premise that we are business allies, offering a supportive hand to help businesses succeed. When my clients are feeling overwhelmed with their workload but are not ready to hire another full-time employee, I can help relieve some of that stress, by catering for their varied needs and allowing them the flexibility to focus on their core business.

> **If you don't go after what you want, you'll never have it. If you don't ask, the answer is always no. If you don't step forward, you're always in the same place.**
> Nora Roberts

Only months after launching Sosocii, I was delighted to discover I was pregnant with my second child. Having grown up with two amazing sisters, I knew I wanted my darling daughter to have a sibling, too. Juggling pregnancy and an active toddler, I continued to push on and get my business name out there by attending various networking events in the evening and joining several online groups before launching my own online networking group, too. The income was minimal throughout this stage, and yet I found myself learning so much. I built my marketing skills, established key connections in the industry and continued to gain a variety of clients.

It was following the birth of my second daughter that my world took the most dramatic turn. After the initial euphoria of bonding with my newborn, watching her connect with her loving big sister and recovering from a caesarean section, everything changed in a day. My partner of twelve years wasn't happy with the life we had created and left the relationship and our family home. Not long later, he revealed he was in a relationship with a former student of his, ten years younger than me.

At just thirty years old, I found myself suddenly single and parenting my newborn and three-year-old daughters. I was overwhelmed with shock and yet my daughters gave me the determination to get up every day. I often survived on merely four hours of broken sleep while navigating the biggest emotional journey of my life. It was my mother who endured hours on the phone listening to me cry and providing the crucial support I needed in the darkest days of my life. Each morning when I'd wake up next to my two precious babies, I knew I had to be strong and I had to keep going for them. They were my world and I had to help forge a positive little universe for them to thrive in. When I found myself looking for some hope, something to push me to get me through the hardest days, I managed to find that in my business. It gave me a drive and excitement that kept my mind active and gave me the intense focus I needed at a crucial time of my life. My business saved me when I felt my world crumbling.

It is impossible to live without failing at something, unless you live so cautiously that you might as well not have lived at all, in which case, you fail by default.
J.K. Rowling

Within the first week of solo parenting, I was already organising a massive rebrand, completely redesigning the Sosocii image with a new logo, website and expanded services. With an increasingly professional appearance, my business seemed to go next level. As soon as the children were asleep, I was on my laptop until the early hours of the morning typing away. I was creating branding content for social media, ghost writing blogs for other businesses, running various online marketing ad campaigns, writing copy for websites and apps. I loved the variety that came with working over several industries. As my business grew and my reputation flourished, so too did the business bank account. I then launched the Melbourne West chapter of Start Up Mum, running free monthly networking events for mums in business and filming a mini class for Start Up Mum on the benefits of outsourcing. It was all the perfect distraction I needed more than anything. I couldn't relax and watch television anyway, so this was a way to be busy, productive and looking to the future for the success I craved.

There's something really empowering about going, 'Hell, I can do this! I can do this all!' That's the wonderful thing about mothers, you can because you must, and you just do.
Kate Winslet

The juggle was extremely challenging at times and then I had the added stress of having to find money to pay out my ex-husband for the home I was raising the children in, as we worked out property settlement. Then, the dreaded family court battles to secure custody arrangements. It was all part of the biggest emotional rollercoaster of my life and as if solo parenting two children, three years and under and running a business wasn't enough to manage, I then decided I had better start renovating the house, too. So, when I wasn't typing away in the evenings, I was busily packing boxes and moving furniture. We were living through re-plastering, painting, reflooring and more, occasionally retreating to my mother's house so we could escape the fumes. Managing trades and renovation timelines on top of everything else seemed like madness to some of my family and friends and yet I pulled it off. One day at a time, one list at a time, oh, and a baby carrier that saved my sanity most days.

I found the biggest appreciation for solo mums. My mum did an amazing job raising three strong women. My sister was a single mum and did an amazing job raising my nephew. I have friends that are raising their children solo, too; some with a support network and others completely on their own. Some have the biological fathers taking children some weekends and others have 100% care, which can be the ultimate win for some, but also means no 'me time' at all for others. I also found that so many of the inspiring business women I was connecting with were or are solo mums achieving absolutely amazing things! It gave me so much joy to see women out their raising their babies and owning their dreams, regardless of societal stigmas.

There's nothing quite like a marriage breakdown to catapult you onto a journey of spiritual discovery and that's exactly where I found myself. I began embracing aromatherapy, meditation and exploring various elements of spiritual healing. I started to learn all about positive manifestation and would fall asleep each evening calling in all of my desires - both within my personal life and in business too. I found this new-found gratitude and positive focus saw me finding all sorts of new and exciting things coming my way. The tide was changing, I was being swept up in an ever-increasing sense of self-confidence and truly embracing the journey.

> **Sometimes things happen to us that we just don't understand. These things sometimes become the doors and windows to our destiny.**
> Andrea Nugent

Having survived the best part of a year, I was well and truly finding my groove. I had finally spent time learning about myself, what I enjoyed, what made me happy and what gave me purpose and drive. I had sworn off men, deciding instead to pursue my ambitions, enjoy financial freedom and focus on raising my daughters into strong self-assured women. My ability to adapt and turn a big negative into a positive made me proud of myself, too. However, after almost a year of solo mumma hustling, I met my current partner Chris, an amazing solo father in his own right. He was working through an incredibly unique situation, having found himself raising his one-year old son by himself, following his ex-partner receiving a terminal cancer diagnosis and consequently leaving the relationship. We seemed to bond almost instantly. Our daily support for each other fostered an incredibly intense connection, soothing each other's ongoing heartache. While I found myself going through the exhausting custody process, he continued to support his son through the process of watching his mother so unwell. He was tragically coming to terms with the fact that his son would grow up without his biological mum in his life. He had also made it clear from the start that I would be taking on a huge role for his son, should our relationship continue, as his son would view me as a mum, especially following the impending passing of his own mother. I knew I had enough love and strength to give them both everything I could to help them now and into the future. Throughout the ups and the downs coming our way, we began to merge our two families into one, moving in together and making a fresh start in the Yarra Valley.

Life with three children, five and under is incredibly busy and yet there is so much beauty, too. The children all get something uniquely positive out of their relationships with each other and with both of us. Our youngest two won't even have memories of the times before they were part of our blended family. They give us endless love and laughs and there is never a dull moment in our house, that's for sure, hence the desire to have the ultimate employment flexibility available through a home-based business. I still do the occasional day relief teaching at local primary schools and I do enjoy it. However, I prefer the days I am home making memories with my babies who are growing each day, then opting to work in the evenings to compensate. It allows me the ultimate balance between family life and my career ambitions, both of which need fulfilling for me to feel complete.

A woman in harmony with her spirit is like a river flowing. She goes where she will without pretense, and arrives at her destination, prepared to be herself and only herself.
Maya Angelou

The wonderful flexibility of an online business allowed me to move from one side of Melbourne to the other and simply continue to provide the same service. That's not to say I haven't had both ups and downs along the way. At times, business cashflow has been an issue. Also, the way clients tend to pull back over Christmas and into the new year, compared to other months. Clients come and go depending on their own business journeys and their own cash flow for outsourcing. Some people don't understand your worth or your prices. I had to understand that they were never going to be in my target market in the first place. It was a journey in embracing what I bring to the table, owning my value and understanding my audience. Some days I have found myself taking setbacks to heart, but then looking for the lesson at hand, breathing and refocusing before moving on. That's when it's important to know your support network. Who's in your corner cheering you on in life? My mum Kerry has always been there for me to bounce my ideas off and to utilise her wealth of business knowledge and skills. Her praise of my ambition sees me striving to try new directions and to kick goals I never thought possible. My partner Chris constantly compliments my drive and supports all of my business dreams. A few months ago, he wrote down messages of love from our children for my birthday and when he asked my eldest daughter about what she thinks of her mummy, she said, "My mum is a hard, good worker at her work. My mum gives me lots of hugs and kisses". It meant so much to me that she knows that I love her, but also that I work hard, too. I hope that I can subtly instill a sense of ambition and drive in them too, so that they may discover what sets their hearts on fire.

If you want to be successful in this world, you have to follow your passion, not a pay check.
Jen Welter

I've learnt to really celebrate the wins throughout my business journey. I was delighted to receive a business scholarship for the Women's Business School earlier this year. I met some incredibly inspiring women whilst continuing to increase my skills and confidence. I then launched a new Start Up Mum chapter in the Yarra Valley and whilst promoting it, I even made it onto Yarra Ranges Life TV.

> **Take every chance you get in life, because some things only happen once.**
> Karen Gibbs

Recently, I was delighted to find out I was a finalist for the 2017 AusMumpreneur Awards and I thoroughly enjoyed the two-day conference in Sydney and the awards gala at Doltone House. I was so happy to meet so many incredible women making a difference across Australia and internationally. I was so inspired by their business journeys and found myself making life-long friends in the process.

Truly feeling at home and content in life, I plan to continue to raise our beautiful children, while working on our businesses. I'll keep running my online networking group with over 900 members and the face to face local business mums group. I plan to continue working on my writing and join a writing academy to continue to foster my creativity whilst refining my skills. I plan to get more sleep but know that's unlikely in the next decade or so...

> **Instead of looking at the past, I put myself ahead twenty years and try to look at what I need to do now to get there.**
> Diana Ross

Well, what doesn't kill you, makes you stronger, right?! It certainly seems that way. It was throughout the last few years of hardship that I really found out who I am, the strength I possess, and it brought me to where I am today! I am so grateful for my wonderful family and the exciting business adventures I'm lucky enough to pursue. I'll always remember that hope, positivity and determination can drive you through life's storms and see you through to happier times. Ultimately, being a mum means the world to me, however it is my business journey that reminds me to reflect on the fact that I am indeed More than a Mum.

Women have to harness their power – it's absolutely true. It's just learning not to take the first no. And if you can't go straight ahead, you go around the corner.

– **Cher**

Bronte Spicer

Soul Worker Academy

When I welcomed meditation into my life, everything changed for me. After a long and debilitating decade of depression, meditation helped me become radically aware of the never-ending stream of unhelpful thoughts my ego created. With this simple, yet profound practice I came to understand these thoughts were an ingrained part of being human that would never leave. I learnt that even though my ego formed these thoughts, it didn't mean there was any substantial truth to them. This was a huge lightbulb moment. With stillness, I could detach my life from those thoughts and consider, 'If I'm not these thoughts, then who am I?'

When I explored my life-long curiosity in spirituality, I discovered my soul beyond my ego's fear-based thoughts and saw clearly that I could either feed this lower-vibrational fear energy or channel divine love into my life. I made it my mission to choose love. My life was transformed from viewing myself as a failure that no one could fix, to a spark of possibility who could follow her dreams.

I began my business when my firstborn, Jackson arrived in 2015. I remember him rocking back-and-forth in the bouncer while I started my online presence on Facebook under the name 'Holistic Living', which then changed to 'Creative Spirit' for a while, as I transitioned my focus from health and wellbeing to spirituality before building Facebook pages Bronte Spicer, Soul Worker Academy, my beloved Facebook group Soul Worker Sisterhood and Instagram account, Bronte Spicer. I was so inspired by my business that I worked at ridiculous hours of the night, too excited to sleep. My business was my other baby and a welcome outlet for the self-love that rumbled from my heart.

I'd been practising Reiki for six years prior and once I secured an affordable space to rent locally with a fellow Reiki Practitioner, this was my first service for both adults and children. I'd attended a two-day Certified Angel Card Reader Workshop with Doreen Virtue and this soon became an additional service for my clients. Following, as I studied with the Australian Centre for Holistic Studies to receive my Advanced Certificate in Guiding and Teaching Meditation, I offered regular meditation courses and workshops, and eventually soul retreats.

Reflecting on this time, my biggest challenge was believing in my services. I began my meditation classes as a casual service, where my clients would pay as they go. Sometimes I would have one person arrive for my classes, and while I presented calmly on the surface, I was riddled with anxiety about how I was going to afford my rent. I was petrified to charge for classes by the term and could only imagine losing all of my students as a result. Reflecting now, my fees were extremely reasonable considering the benefits my students were experiencing, yet I was blind to the true value of my classes.

I realised I was doing my students a disservice by offering casual meditation classes because the fee structure didn't encourage them to practice regularly. The more they attended my classes the calmer, more centered and energised they felt. I saw a huge spike in commitment levels from my students when I replaced casual fees with term fees. Similarly, with Reiki treatments, initially I refrained from suggesting to my clients who really needed it, to return for a second or even third treatment in case they interpreted this gesture as revenue-building. When I remembered the purpose of my service - to help my clients to be the healthiest and most vibrant version of themselves - it was my responsibility to put my own limiting story aside and offer them the support they needed.

Taking courageous action improved my service for my clients and helped me pay the rent too!

It was at this time that my mindset around my business income started to shift in a welcomed direction; I was making money! I felt inspired to map out my projected income and felt a sense of pride when I could pay my rent with ease. I began contributing to the family's spending money and invested 50% of the gross profits back into the business. I always had an inkling that my work would be wildly successful, and it was exciting to see the start of the fruits of my labour.

Soon after, my sense of trust in my vision was tested. I'd been doing the odd day of casual relief teaching (CRT) at my old school which comparatively, was good money for our family. In order to be available for CRT I had to limit my appointments for my clients. I grew frustrated with CRT, often not receiving work when I'd turned down appointments with my clients. Despite the lure of good money from CRT, I had to dig deep and fiercely trust that if I kept myself available for my clients, my business would grow and surpass the income CRT offered. This part of my journey tested how committed and dedicated I was to my soul work... thankfully, I passed.

As more clients came for readings, I witnessed an influx of people who wanted a career change and had a quiet desire to run a business doing what they loved. I thrived on sharing the intuitive wisdom that was channeled for these clients and could see it was a direct reflection of my own journey. I realised this was my passion; to support and inspire others to trust their intuition enough to follow their heart and pursue the work of their soul.

A part of me felt somewhat limited sharing my work in one-on-one appointments. I wanted to inspire more women and make a bigger impact. A teacher by trade, I wanted to show thousands of women how meditation could change their lives, how to channel age-old wisdom so they could lift themselves out of the illusion of their worries, stop believing those nasty fear-based thoughts and return to their truth; that they are an incredible bundle of infinite possibility and they can create their wildest dreams.

I wanted to create a ripple effect of love right across the globe.

A vehicle for growth in my own self-worth, I knew that I needed to invest in some coaching to help me get my message out to more women. In the past, I had found it impossible to invest in my business; it took me six long years to buy $200 annual insurance for my Reiki services. 'What if it doesn't all work out?' I doubted... 'What if I spend all this money and my business is a failure?' I came to a realisation that I was worth spending money on, that I was worthy of receiving my dreams and that I had the choice to invest in my big vision. Once I raised my self-worth and began to invest in my business, my income grew faster than ever.

I took baby steps with my investments in coaching. I balked at the price for a package of two coaching calls with Cosmic Alchemist and Brand Whisperer, Eloise Meskanen, but something deep within me was calling me to work with her... so I did. Months later, I took the plunge and signed up for Kushla Chadwick's Confident Coach Academy, to learn how to enrol more clients in a heart-centred way. When I registered to work with Kushla, I couldn't quite work out what I was doing... I was signing up for something I couldn't afford! I only had enough money for the first instalment and had no idea how I was going to cover the rest of the payments. Again, something deep within was calling me to step up and be a part of this academy. I was learning quickly to follow my guidance in order to manifest my dreams, and of course, I received more than enough money to pay for the Confident Coach Academy.

Having someone coach me accelerated my path to my dreams as a Spiritual Entrepreneur. In just weeks, I had channeled the SOUL Method and the Soul Worker Academy, I was clear on who my clients were, and I knew what my gifts and talents were. I could see which problems I could help my clients solve, I knew how to market my services and sell my program in a way that didn't feel icky. In the words of Soul Leader Mentor Melissa Sandon, I had embodied the feeling that I was 'that woman' who had a business coach.

My business evolved into a sacred path of service in total alignment with my soul. Now, I help women on a spiritual path who have a deep yearning to serve. They want to help and care for people and the planet. I refer to them as 'Soul Workers', because they work from the essence of their soul, or love. Maybe you really want to help people feel healthy and well through yoga and nutrition or show others how to become mentally resilient with meditation and Emotional Freedom Technique (EFT) or teach children how to practice loving kindness through picture stories.

If you have a strong desire to help others, then you are a Soul Worker.

I founded the Soul Worker Academy; an online learning facility that guides Spiritual Entrepreneur Mums to build a solid connection to their soul and higher purpose, courageously step into their role of leadership as an expert in their field and follow their path of service, all while making a healthy income for themselves and their family. I define Spiritual Entrepreneur Mums as Mums who run a business that's in alignment with their soul purpose. Loss of identity can be rife in motherhood when we are thrown into the role of feeding around the clock, cleaning, changing nappies, washing, drying, shopping and the rest. Since you're reading this book, it's likely that you dream of running your own business. Maybe you envision yourself running health retreats or writing books or speaking for TED, sharing your powerful message. The Soul Worker Academy is for those women who have done the study and need to learn to manage the relentless fears and self-sabotage that can feel crippling in the journey of entrepreneurship. It gives you a pathway to help people you're truly inspired to, unlock your ultimate potential and manifest your wildest dreams.

The Soul Worker Academy supports you to build:

* confidence in your gifts, experience and abilities
* trust in your intuition and;
* competence in running a successful business.

What I have learnt, is that when you are clear about your abilities and gifts, you can accelerate yourself to your dreams in business. Throughout your life, or lives, you collect skills, wisdom and abilities through study, professional and personal experience and when these are ignited by the work of your soul, they become your powerful set of soul gifts. The Soul Worker Academy helps Mums find clarity on what their soul gifts are and who they're specifically passionate about working with, to then create tangible soul offerings that ignite their fire. When you have the pleasure of fulfilling your purpose and potential, that's when you get to experience true abundance.

While observing the women I worked with, I realised their biggest struggle was trusting their intuition and brilliant ideas they were receiving to make the positive impact they dreamt of. This led me to birth the SOUL Method. The SOUL Method is a framework to move out of constantly worrying and doubting yourself, to build a strong abundance mindset, return to the infinite possibility that you are, receive clear steps from the universe and practice courage to leap with faith and take solid action towards your dreams as an entrepreneur.

The SOUL Method is comprised of four elements:

S – See the Truth
O – Open and Expand
U – Unite with Consciousness
L – Leap with Faith.

See the Truth. When you're in alignment with your soul, you see the truth; your soul is a part of the collective consciousness and all that is, you are infinite possibility and can create what you desire. Yet when your reality is swayed by the ego's fear-based thinking, you are living within the illusion of fear. Maybe you haven't started your business because you feel you don't know enough, despite having undergone study at great lengths or even had professional experience in your proposed field. Perhaps you can't see past all the things that could go wrong with your business or you might doubt you can make a good income from what you really want to do. These are all fears from your ego and not the voice of your soul. You are a spiritual being having a human experience and the truth is that you are qualified enough, things will go right, and you can make a good income from the work you yearn to pursue. By unraveling each layer of resistance or limitation encasing your soul, you allow more of your potential to birth into your world. As you begin to implement techniques like meditation, journaling and affirming on a daily basis, you can realign with your soul and see the truth in every situation. The commitment you show when dedicating yourself to a daily sacred practice offers trust in the universe and courage like no other to act upon the ideas and guidance you receive.

Open and Expand. You have an energetic body as well as a physical body, which acts as a gateway to connect with your infinite potential. If you have practiced yoga or had a Reiki treatment, you're likely to be aware of the chakric system. Each chakra, or spinning wheel of energy creates flow, offering balance and vitality in the body, mind and soul. Learning to channel fresh, new energy into your body offers you the opportunity to channel your desires. The soulful business that you crave, the income that you dream of, the inspiring work that you envision yourself doing and the impact you see yourself making all emit a particular vibration. As you look after your energetic body through energy-healing, meditation and other energy work, you can attract the vibration of your dream business and it inevitably manifests into form. Now, the universe will not hand you your dreams on a platter without commitment and action. Yet, energy work is a powerful tool to build your belief mindset and trust in your path to your life as a successful entrepreneur. Experiencing the expansive nature of your energy field quickly reminds you there is more than the physical world you live in, there is more at play than what the eye can see, you are unlimited potential and your dream business is possible.

Unite with Consciousness. When you unite with the collective consciousness you have the delectable experience of connecting to your soul guidance and receiving your next action step to take towards your dreams. Your soul guidance is the team of spiritual beings that have been assigned to you in this lifetime to help you fulfill your soul purpose. They might include guides, angels, ascended masters, animal spirit guides, gods, goddesses, deities and fairies. Infusing automatic journaling, card readings, prayer and meditation into your sacred practice develops your four intuitive abilities, including clairvoyance, clairsentience, claircognizance and clairaudience.

These help you receive clear messages and learn to trust the guidance enough to follow through with action. Intuitive messages from your soul guidance can come in various forms for your business such as synchronicities, recurring numbers, new ideas or symbolic dreams at night. Learning how to receive clear messages from the universe can be a powerful tool as an entrepreneur because you are always making decisions. When you are tuned into your soul you can learn to choose from love rather than fear. Your soul guidance always guides you back to love and will support you on your path to your highest visions as a Soul Worker.

Leap with Faith. When you take the plunge to leap with faith you are practicing full trust in the universe that it is safe for you to implement the action you've been guided to take. Perhaps you're getting the call to speak at a local community event, apply to be a guest on a podcast or become a published writer. The students of the Soul Worker Academy are guided to take action within what I refer to as the 'Magic Zone' and this is crucial to creating your dreams and desires. In order for magic to happen, you need to step out of your comfort zone. Concurrently, it's important that you don't push yourself too far beyond your limits that you shut down. You need to take action that excites you and brings nerves along with it, too. You also need to take action that gives you enough space to manage the fears that arise with it. If you choose an action that is far greater than you can handle, you will bypass magic and enter overwhelm. Your role as a Soul Worker is to remain curious enough to observe how far love will take you, implement your action steps and let go of the outcome, surrender to the divine nature of the universe and maintain faith that your guidance has heard your desires. Sometimes what you receive is just as you'd envisioned and other times it's a blessing in disguise. A Soul Worker practices trust that they are exactly where they need to be, and everything is in divine order.

Throughout the thirteen modules of the Soul Worker Academy, women build an unwavering faith in their abilities to create a business that's aligned with what their soul desires. It initiates powerful healing, builds a sacred practice, deepens an awareness of Self and naturally penetrates self-love and self-fulfillment into their lives. They journey through a process of releasing the shackles that hold them back and begin to express who they truly are with the world. I am blessed to witness the profound personal growth and wild transformation of the women who journey through the Soul Worker Academy.

Taking action as if I was already successful made huge changes for me on my path to running a successful business. I used to compare myself to other entrepreneurs, see their websites with their beautiful photos and think 'I'm not good enough to have photos like that taken. They must have a massive income to be able to afford that'. When I caught myself saying that, I questioned it, 'What's really stopping me from having beautiful photos and a professional website?' My mindset shifted, and I was quick to trade some Soul Coaching sessions for the most immaculate professional shots from local photographer Lou Firli and this helped me believe in the successful progression of my business. As I welcomed my fears and took action in the presence of the divine, my soul work continued to grow.

Once I'd learnt the nuts-and-bolts of business, I knew I needed more time to implement the strategies. I'd been limiting my time spent on my business to the bare-minimum in the fear that I was asking my husband for too much and that I was neglecting my children. After really considering what the truth was in this situation, I realised that my yearning to do this work was so big that I couldn't live without it. I had a deep and heart-felt responsibility to help more people to see what was possible for them. So, I thought, 'I might as well make some money while I'm at it'. I had been spending some time away from my family to work on my business. If I spent a little more time, I could keep filling my cup and make a good income for the family. This is when it dawned on me that my business could be uber-successful. Together, we got accountable with my two-days of work per week at home. I got dressed up to go to 'work' in the back room of our house. It was the first time I took my business seriously. I made a decision to become a wildly abundant entrepreneur and this kept me on-track, ensuring I was utilizing my work hours in the most productive way to grow my business.

That year, with my second-born, Ivy just a few months old, I made more money than I ever dreamed of through my soul work.

Building a healthy income from my business gave me more inspiration to share what I had learnt about business with fellow Spiritual Entrepreneur Mums. I knew what it was like to doubt my own abilities to create an abundant business from the work that I loved, and I wanted to show every other Soul Worker how they could move out of doubt and build their dream business too. I included the modules 'Monetise Your Soul Work' and 'Embed and Embody Your Soul Work' in the Soul Worker Academy, which are jam-packed with ways to market and sell with soul. If I could make a good income, so could my clients.

One of the biggest worries my clients have is, 'What will they think of me?' and maybe this is a fear of yours, too. Being spiritual can feel foreign to the mainstream Australian culture and it took courage for me to stand up and express this deeply-felt part of me. You might feel different in some way or feel as though if you shared who you truly are, and what your actual dreams are, you might be ridiculed. On my journey of choosing love, I have expressed more of who I truly am, and my self-expression has been both warmly received and utterly rejected. Both have been a blessing. The more you share your truth, the more you calibrate with your tribe. When you are rejected by family or friends, it is a blessing for you to raise these big fears of yours to the surface. I have been called 'fake' and my work has been labelled 'bullshit'. While I initially felt hurt by these words, it encouraged me to really question these deep-seated fears of mine. 'Am I fake?' or 'Have I been brainwashed?' Sitting with these raw feelings and exploring these fears, I came to a deeper understanding that this was my path, and not for anyone else. Other people may not understand my journey of full self-expression, but I am choosing love and pursuing my dreams.

As you step further into your potential and experience rejection yourself, practice a healthy dose of self-awareness and self-compassion. Becoming radically present with the unhelpful thoughts your ego creates like, 'No one's going to buy it', 'You're not good enough', or 'You're never going to make it' is crucial. In fact, write them down in your journal so you can extract them from your monkey mind. If you have a healthy connection with the universe, call in the wisdom of your soul and ask, 'What is the truth in this situation?' and finally, wrap pure divine, white light around your body and into your heart as you feel the anger, pain, frustration, sadness or any other uncomfortable emotion that arises. Let yourself feel into the discomfort that comes with rejection and love yourself anyway. A tangible toolkit to manage your thoughts and emotions is key to being successful in business.

Practicing balance in your life helps you avoid burnout and create longevity. As an entrepreneur, I choose to be in the game for the long haul, so I must ensure I'm balancing work, family and time for myself. Early in my business, I worked solidly each night as soon as I could.

Initially, I was naturally inspired, but this quickly turned into the grind, like I was a slave to the never-ending to-do list for my business. My ego kept pushing me to WORK. WORK. WORK. A couple of times, I fell in a heap, as sick as a dog and unable to feel any natural desire to be immersed in my work; I was out of soul alignment. I needed to create boundaries for myself, so I didn't feel like my entire life was work.

I implemented clear boundaries to express my truth for myself, my family and my business:

- Accept your work will never finish. There will always be more to do, and it doesn't all need to happen overnight. Strengthen your trust in divine timing and know that in order to fulfill your soul purpose, you don't need to be working like a crazy lady.

- Don't work at night. Spend time with your loved ones and immerse yourself in your sacred practice. Read. Go to yoga.

- Don't work on your days off. While it's easy to be productive with a three-month old bouncing away in the bouncer, it's a mental nightmare to try and work on your business as your children get older. Enjoy your precious time with your children. Be present with them, engage with them, marvel in their beauty and have fun with them.

Building a dream is a team-effort. Lisa Forde, Principal of the Australian Centre for Holistic Studies is my mentor and I am always looking for additional coaches to help me on my path. My husband is my biggest supporter of my dreams. We are lucky enough he is home from shift work for seven days a fortnight and is with the kids while I work. I've hired others to help with babysitting, marketing and administration along the way. You're not meant to do it all alone, so reach out for the help you need.

Life as an entrepreneur is a journey of profound personal growth and self-development. Since running my own business, I feel empowered to make my dreams a reality. I believe in myself and know I offer something worthwhile. I continue to become clearer on what my soul gifts are, and I have gained confidence in sharing my work. I know the value of my soul offerings and I'm comfortable in inviting my soul clients to work with me. Each time I take the next step, whether it's a leap or tiny shuffle, I am reclaiming more of my innate power to express who I am with the world and it's truly liberating.

My path as a Spiritual Entrepreneur Mum continues to unfold. I am excited to be currently writing my own book, a sacred guidebook filled with spiritual practices, intuitive wisdom, energy rituals, meditations and more to accelerate you on your path to your wildest dreams as a Spiritual Entrepreneur Mum. I would love to co-create some oracle cards to accompany this book to help you develop your trust in your intuition even further. And, I am looking forward to adding the Soul Worker Retreat to the Soul Worker Academy, a nourishing in-person experience where you can dig deep into your soul, release what no longer serves you and find the courage to take that next big leap.

If I had some final words of wisdom for you, as a Mum with a dream to start your own business, it would be to rebuild your beliefs around how you can generate an income for you and your family. Gone are the days where financial security must come from a 9-5 job. You live in an exciting time where you can reach your clients right across the globe from the comfort of your own home. Facebook alone has two billion active users. Ditch the old employment paradigm and enter the new. Contrary to what some people believe, it is possible for you to build a business through the work of your soul.

From my heart to yours,

Ellen Lorraine Niemeier

Soul-Level Healing LLC

My name is Ellen Lorraine Niemeier. I'm a single mom of a beautiful three-year-old son and I own my own business, Soul-Level Healing LLC. It was a bit of a bumpy ride to get here. There are certain things I've known for as long as I can remember. I always knew I wanted to create my own business — I started my first one when I was eleven, doing cleaning projects for $1.00/hour. Before that, I was already drawing up inventions and writing stories. I knew I wanted to play the violin, not even sure I had ever heard one before, but I *knew* without a doubt that I needed to play one. Finally, after many delays, I began taking lessons when I was ten years old.

I was a sensitive kid, picking up easily on the emotions of others. I was never one who could witness a friend cry and not start crying too (I'm still like that today). I had highly detailed dreams, many of which were foretelling in some way. Sometimes they would give me a heads up about a big change ahead, and other times just small, minute details would come through and turn out to be part of my day the next day.

I recall sitting under a tree in our back yard when I was about eight years old and feeling very peaceful singing and reading and just *being* outside. That image has come to me many times in recent days, accompanied by a feeling of peace and contentedness.

I was the kind of person who always knew exactly what she wanted to do. I had this strong sense that I was going to die young, like by my mid-thirties, so I made ambitious goals for myself (it turns out that I died young in my last lifetime). I wanted to study music, but also help people, so I got into college for music therapy and French (I also always knew I wanted to live in France and I had a sense that I needed to be able to speak to people who could not speak English). I studied abroad to France, again, after several set-backs. Finally, the right program, the finances, and everything came together when I was twenty-two.

I worked really hard in high school and college. I started another few businesses in high school: cleaning homes (this time for a regular market fee) when I was fourteen, teaching violin lessons when I was sixteen, and playing in a professional string quartet on violin when I was seventeen. I also worked in restaurants and retail stores, as well as managing a hefty load of school work and chores.

I moved away to go to college, from St. Louis, Missouri, to Fort Collins, Colorado. I took 10-12 classes per semester and worked in photo labs, restaurants, and then got into teaching pre-school and English as a second language to kids of all ages. I also started my cleaning business again locally, and it built quickly with word of mouth. I knew that I wanted to create my own thing when I was finished with school. I was doing exactly what I wanted and what I set my mind to in college, but I still longed for a sense of freedom and abundance.

I finished school and started a music therapy business to assist with stress reduction for teens and adults. The idea was to use drumming to meet everyone right where they were and let off excess energy in the drumming until everyone reached a place of calmness and possibly even joy, and then to slow things down using soft, calming music to facilitate a guided progressive muscle relaxation, all while using breathing to achieve a more relaxed state. It was a brilliant idea, and I was able to find places that would allow me to host groups for free, so long as I invited the residents there. I had clients signing up and it was so exciting! But then, bam! I injured my lower back working with an un-trained personal trainer. My perfect plan of teaching little kiddos part-time (I taught one-year olds), while building my business was dashed. I could barely walk, let alone pick up the kids to change diapers. The income dried up, so even offering change to folks coming to my group music therapy sessions was next to impossible; not to mention my back injury made activities like carrying things or driving difficult, so even leading a session was becoming out of the question. I was so disappointed and ashamed.

I felt like I had asked everyone to have faith in me and my ideas, only to let everyone down and find myself in a position of needing help to get on my feet again.

I decided to apply for music therapy jobs all over the U.S. and I got one in New York! I had five days to pack up and get there! I had help, as my back was still healing. I arrived in New York, met my dad who moved to NYC when I was in college, and got acquainted with the area. I started my new job and was told shortly after I arrived, that the position was nearly cut while I was driving from Colorado to New York! My boss saved the day, explaining that it had been filled and I was literally in transit to take the position. Phew.

The job itself was fulfilling in some regards. I loved witnessing miracles with people. What a joy to sing with someone who had not spoken for years. How awesome to walk with people who were not able to walk independently (but could with music and assistance). The residents were beautiful and changed my heart in so many ways. But at the same time, my heart yearned for something more. I wasn't sure what exactly; it was nearly impossible to put into words just why I wasn't feeling content as a music therapist. After all, I'd studied for seven years to achieve what I had and was incredibly well-qualified. It was exactly what I wanted - using music every single day and helping people. Yet, there was something missing...

This was the point where I went on a long, winding, wild-goose chase in my career. I knew I had transferrable skills and decided to try my hand in business, in the corporate arena. I started out doing human resources and marketing for a large non-profit. I enjoyed the work but found myself drained by the environment. I got tired of having great work being stolen by people ahead of me in rank and presented as their own. I got tired of the ego and the idea that doing things ethically wasn't important. I was exhausted from trying to fit into a box, with parameters defined by someone else. And, this was just the first job I'd taken outside of music! I then got into sales, first in the dental industry, then in insurance. Naturally, when networking, I was *always* attracted to the wellness people in the room. There could have been 200 people at an event with 197 of those people in banking, insurance, law, or taxes. I would meet the three who had some kind of holistic healing or wellness business, without fail. We would just find each other. And, *lots* of other Ellen's as a funny side-note. I recall one event where there were eighteen women, and nine of us were Ellen's! Anyway.

I was trying *so hard* to make this selling insurance thing my 'thing', the thing that was going to get me into lots of money, freedom and happiness.

But alas, I found that not only was I drained, I was disheartened because I didn't care about what I was doing at *all* – not at a soul-level. Heck, not even at a heart-level. I met lovely people, however. I had tons of potential clients come to me because they could trust me, or they connected with me because I played violin in local orchestras, or some other 'something' they just liked. I really wanted it to be my thing. I was thrilled when I was offered a great position with a successful firm, complete with an office with a view, and you know what happened? I was fired. Why? I was told that I was too gentle in spirit, too 'nice', and that if an obstacle was in my way, I wasn't the type of person to bulldoze it over. I tried gently to explain that you can walk around an obstacle peacefully and still find success, but of course, that didn't help the negotiation to keep the job. I had never been fired. I always had excellent reviews everywhere I worked. I was so ashamed. I didn't apply for unemployment, because I felt like that would be telling the Universe I was unemployed. I had so much resistance inside me against this, and I just felt like giving up. I was hired by another agency, on commission only, which helped me get some sense of esteem back, and I worked with some lovely people, but it was the last job in insurance I ever took.

Two events took place that changed things forever. The first, was a gentle whisper from a friend. I had just gotten onto Facebook and was delighted to find my friends from my year in France! A dear friend of mine was getting married in Spain that summer, and he asked me to 'play my violin so loudly, that they could hear it all the way from New York'. It woke me up. I could not believe he remembered I played violin and that it *meant* something to someone. It was a spark in my heart, that reminded me that before I got on the bandwagon of trying super hard to be someone I wasn't, that I had passion for things in my life! And violin was one of those things! The second event occurred when I flew on a plane to my mother's wedding. When I arrived in St. Louis, I closed my eyes and had this strong message come through, that I needed to move back to St. Louis, where I had left twelve years prior.

Once I made up my mind to follow the Divine guidance received to move back to St. Louis, it only took a couple of weeks to pack up my little car, sell most of my belongings and hit the road. I had been feeling miserable and lost, and this step – though totally into the unknown – felt decisive.

It felt like I was doing something to change my life.

After I moved, I made bold choice after bold choice. I say 'bold' because these choices were not celebrated by my family or even all my friends. They didn't come with an outcome already mapped out. They came with pure faith as I was leaping into the unknown time and again. First, I turned down a very nice job offer with an insurance firm. I would have done supremely well at the job itself but felt strongly that it wasn't the way to go to change my life, so I turned it down. I took jobs that were closer to my interests, but all of them had long waits before I got them.

Lots of time passed and I was feeling like things wouldn't work out. My car was repossessed. I had the landlord banging on my door demanding rent. It surely wasn't yet the life I had envisioned for myself!

Another turning point came when a friend asked me to play violin for her wedding. I was so honored, and I wanted to *so* badly, but truth be told, I hadn't touched my violin in over a year, I was feeling ashamed at what my skill level must have been like with the lack of practice, and ultimately, I didn't play in her wedding. She was gracious about it, but I was secretly dying inside. *How could I just let my gifts go to waste? How could I just meet my goals and live with so much purpose only until I was about 25, then let it all go?* I decided right then that I wasn't going to be that person. I wasn't going to have an 'Oh, when I was younger...' storyline forever. I was going to bite the bullet and get some assistance and bawl my eyes out practicing my violin for as long as it would take to feel good about it again. I used some grocery money a family member was giving me to get lessons, and dedicated time daily to practice, and many tears did flow. However, it was not very long until things started to change.

Just two short months after starting lessons to brush up, I was accepted into a graduate school program for music. On the second day of school, I was offered a teaching job that paid significantly more than I was earning at the catering job I had at the time. The same day, my mom offered to co-sign on a loan, so I could get a car again and be able to take the amazing job offer. And, within a month, I was hired to play a gig at a wedding, where I met my son's father, and in two short weeks, I was pregnant.

Of course, I had already met his father in a dream a few weeks previous. It was so detailed and so real, I *knew* it was him when he introduced himself to me at this wedding. And I *knew* that big change was coming; I had felt that for months, to the point I'd wake up in the middle of the night feeling I needed to prepare for something. But, I wasn't sure what. I was about to find out!

It was a whirlwind romance and I was completely swept off my feet. We felt so comfortable around each other. By the time my feet hit the ground, I was pregnant, and he was *gone*! Just gone. He blocked my phone number, blocked me on social media, and he was evicted from his apartment, so just totally gone.

This experience was certainly a catalyst for healing. I took this opportunity of feeling completely devastated and facing every single fear I'd ever faced all at the same time, to seek support by whatever means had ever captured my attention. I was already seeing an acupuncturist regularly, and she also practiced pranic healing, which was amazing. I cannot quantify the shifts that took place from each of these healings. Not to mention, I had had four physicians tell me I would have a very hard time, if not impossible time trying to conceive. Wrong! Looking back though, even though I hadn't been receiving the acupuncture due to that prognosis, it did help to heal those channels in my body and energy system.

I had a friend that I met at a networking event in New York, and all I knew was that she offered healing. I wasn't even sure what she really did, I just knew in my heart that it was time to explore it, and time to seek the support. She read Akashic Records. Before the first reading, we had just caught up enough that she knew I was expecting, but we didn't really get further than that. The reading was incredible. The longings of my heart were right there. It moved back the veil, so I could see the truth, and also gain the insight from other lifetimes and parts of myself I might not always be aware of. I also got to know my baby's soul before he was even born!

As the pregnancy went on, I became more and more aware of an inner conflict brewing. I wanted to be with my baby, yet I also needed to support us financially. I was teaching orchestra part-time, but even getting a sitter for a few hours a day felt like too much, not to mention the financial consideration there! I applied for a graduate assistantship, where I could work from home, and I got it! At the time, I was still planning to teach.

I really felt torn, like I felt I 'had' to keep that job, but my heart was saying, 'be with your baby'.

I took leaps of faith during the pregnancy as well. I fired my obstetrician at 35 weeks and hired a homebirth midwife (not knowing how I would pay her), deciding this was not a time to settle. I had already hired a doula, knowing that I'd need extra support. I had my beautiful baby boy at home, just a couple of weeks later.

Things got real. Real, deep love and connection to my son. Absolute zero tolerance for bullshit. The greatest joy, the least rest, the deepest guilt, the greatest fears. Great triumphs balanced with the deepest feeling of failure ever experienced. Letting go. I got to have the home birth, and that was the most amazing day of my life; it was like having angels follow me around and support me in gentle whisper while I birthed my baby. I had such amazing energy workers and healers working with me up to this time. "Nothing hides the light and truth of bringing a new life into this world", was my spirit guide's message. I had grown so confident and comfortable being pregnant, where even though I had fears about how to support us, I knew he was perfectly cared for in my belly. I took good care of myself, so he received excellent care. I knew he had plenty to eat, he had a peaceful environment, and he was surrounded by love. I spoke to him often and was aware of him 24 hours a day. When he was born, he spontaneously nursed within his first hour of life. It was beautiful and perfect.

But, within a couple of days, my happy, calm baby, was fussy. And yellow. He wasn't nursing the way he started, and suddenly my feeling of joy was more a feeling of desperation to feed my child. I couldn't leave my apartment because there were super steep steps to get in and out, and I couldn't do that yet. I had limited funds. I was alone with a baby. My midwife felt for me and did go to the store for me, but she wasn't familiar with formula or with bottles, and frankly, I felt like such a failure, I was too embarrassed to even ask her to buy some bottles for me. I also knew that I didn't like the commercial formulas available, but I didn't want my baby to be hungry. More than anything, I didn't want him to be hungry. I was so frustrated he wouldn't nurse! The milk was there! Perfect and there for him! What was worse, was that I was so sleep deprived, I couldn't even hear my own inner voice! I was used to basing *all* of my decisions and finding *all* of the solutions with intuition. And suddenly, the only voices audible were everyone else's.

When he was just four days old, I got a phone call at 1:00am, telling me that his bilirubin levels were double that of what they should be, and that we needed to get to a hospital right away. I couldn't drive, I couldn't really do the steps yet, and more than anything, I did *not* want to go to the hospital. I wanted my baby to have a gentle entrance to life and going to a hospital was not in my view of what I wanted for him. I was devastated, not to mention frozen with all the to-do's just to get us there. It was a holiday weekend, so people weren't in town. My midwife called my doula for me, and she was lovely enough to come get us and take us to the hospital in the middle of the night. She stayed with me until we were admitted to a room.

I have never felt anger the way I did with the first doctors and nurses we met to start the process. I felt like they took something angelic and sacred and tarnished it. It was if suddenly, no divine perfection was 'allowed', and we needed to adopt the fears that the protocols are based on. We had no visitors during our four-day stay. The nurses were amazing once we were admitted, and had questions about home birth, as they were considering it too. I had hospital staff come in to talk with me, and we'd cry together. Part of my soul energy is to hold space of non-judgement, and it shows up by people I barely know, sharing their deepest pains and stories with me. Those were the beautiful moments when we were there. I was also trying to pump and feeling worse and worse about my ability to feed my baby while I was there. The doctor on staff was no help in that regard. "Just give him formula, it won't kill him." Um, but I had breast milk with me from other moms who gave it to us (which I used even though the doctor was a negative-nelly about my desires to give my son breast milk).

We finally got to go home when he was eight days old. He was past the jaundice, which was a blessing. That was an easy blessing to see. But, I felt alone, and I was indeed home alone with a baby. My hopes for a gentle intro to life had been dashed. I wanted to go back and foresee things to change how they were done which of course, is impossible. I was well-prepared; I did my best. I was there for my son. But at the time, I just felt bad. About everything. I felt I had failed at my biggest goal for us, so it felt like a surprise that I got to get up each new day and keep trying.

Another catalyst for healing. I could not go on with the guilt and bad feelings. That was not helping anyone. I wanted to enjoy my son. I wanted to enjoy feeding him. I wanted to reclaim the divine magic of bringing this beautiful life into the world.

I made decisions. I decided to feed him with donated milk. I did pump and nurse as possible but decided to learn a baby-led bottle-feeding method and just let it be our perfect way. I learned about EFT Tapping - Emotional Freedom Technique Tapping to work through the guilt. I would tap during my shower, so I could wash the feelings away down the drain and cry as hard as needed to release it. (I also learned to take that shower the second baby was asleep, as the opportunity didn't always last very long!) After six weeks, I decided to return the pump rental, and stop feeling badly at all about nursing. I researched goat's milk formulas and learned how to make a homemade formula with ingredients I felt really good about. I felt like I could feel joyous in providing that to my baby, and to my delight, he loved it!

As we got closer to the school year starting, I was becoming less and less willing to compromise on my time with my baby. I was able to work from home with the assistantship and bring baby to any meetings as needed (by the way, it's *so* sweet to see your babe sleeping on the shoulder of your boss). I read the contract for the upcoming year for teaching, and subs weren't allowed since it was a part-time gig. I decided that was not flexible enough for us, so I resigned that position. It felt scary, but right at the same time. I started working with my healer friend again, garnering wisdom from the Akashic Records to get some clarity on my purpose and what I really wanted to do in this life. The last decision was crucial to supporting the change I wanted to see.

During this time, I really solidified my desire to be a healer, to let that be my life's work. It also became crystal clear that I was not going to compromise on being a mother and being there for my baby. It was through this journey into motherhood, that the reality that there are no do-overs, so follow your heart *now*, really hit home. I wanted to learn to read the Akashic Records, as these readings had been so helpful to me. The Universe was into it too, and boom, I had an ad in my face on Facebook, to take a course to learn to read them! It was a decision I didn't have to think over, so I signed up right away. Then, I continued on to learn more. I started my business, Soul-Level Healing, LLC, set up my website, and started offering readings worldwide.

I loved that I could serve others, while honoring my schedule with my then, nine-month-old son.

I'd love to say that from that moment forward all was easy-breezy-apple-peezy, but let's face it, following your heart and manifesting the magical life you're determined to create doesn't always happen in a straight line. I learned in the insurance industry, if you're not getting some bumps and bruises along the way, you're not taking adequate action. Hardly comforting when you're in the midst of bumps and bruises while you figure things out.

My state of financial health continued to be an ongoing concern and seeming hurdle to overcome. We had state aid for food and other necessities. I took an expensive loan to help with expenses during the first few months of

Antonio's life. I started to feel a crushing pressure to earn more income, while also feeling huge resistance to doing so away from my baby. I entered a relationship with someone I had been involved with many years ago. It provided for us in many ways, but ultimately was not a healthy connection for me. I needed to leave and in a hurry with very few resources.

Leaps of faith...*so* many leaps of faith in the last three years. I chose to leave St. Louis and stay with friends all over the country for a few days at a time. (When we left St. Louis, I had just enough money to get us to the first stop!) About four weeks into that adventure, my heart knew that Loveland, Colorado was where our new home would be. We found a house-share that worked very temporarily, then again, moved without resources. This time, we were certifiably homeless, with just enough funds for a hotel room for a few days. We stayed with a friend's dad, then in a program for homeless families where we stayed in church classrooms.

At that point, I knew I had to let go and get child care, and get a paycheck coming in. I found a lovely home daycare, after a month and a half of searching and interviewing. It was worth the wait. My son and I both cried for the first two weeks when I dropped him off. It was so hard, but so necessary. I could not be all things to all people and trying to do it all myself was not sustainable anymore. I subbed in the local school district, while I continued to offer readings. During this time, I also started free-lance professional violin performing in the local area. As hard as it was, it was impressive to see what is possible when you decide to do something. I found pretty places to drive to, to sit and meet with my clients on the phone. I made arrangements with volunteers, churches, and friends to babysit, to take violin gigs. I did readings for myself both in the Akasha, and with angel cards to maintain my connection to the spiritual realm and easily hear the divine guidance coming through for me.

We got our new apartment just after Christmas that year. It was the best present ever.

Things got easier once we had a home. I was able to offer more readings and play more gigs. And, it was all so much easier when I could simply hire a sitter to come to our home to watch my son. No one else to coordinate with. I started to feel better about myself as we weren't leaning so much on the community to get on our feet.

Soon enough, subbing didn't feel as aligned with my soul as it had. I felt like I was saving the day for everyone else, when what I wanted to do was save the day for us! Create the magical life that I was so determined to create! And serve others in a meaningful way! And as it happens, the Universe opened a space. It all perfectly fell apart. Sub jobs fell through at the last minute. The childcare I had set up ended abruptly. Sub jobs that were set up, were canceled unexpectedly.

As my seemingly perfect back-up plan crumbled right in front of me, I became aware that I just had enough of back-up plans. Of having a job that others could feel comfortable with. Of barely scraping by, while working really hard all the time. I made the decision to stop reaching for the life-saver and instead, place all of my energy on raising my son and building my business. I invested in myself, got organised, and gave myself permission to serve others with the gifts I have to offer in a big way. No more playing small.
Now, I offer signature programs to serve clients I love working with. I get to use this amazing transformational

energy of the Akashic Records and serve others on their journeys to healing, wholeness and love. I get to peek behind the veil between worlds and gain insight about why our souls chose to come together in this lifetime. I get to read for children! I get to witness profound transcendence and transformation.

Had I taken the much, much easier route of staying in a comfort zone, settling for jobs that were only sort of tolerable, for salaries that kept us just meeting our needs – trading off the time my heart wanted with my baby son – I wouldn't have gotten to experience this. I wouldn't have gotten to meet the beautiful souls that I get to work with. I wouldn't have gotten to offer service that reminds me every single day of our Divinity and the perfection of it all. I wouldn't have learned to thank the hard times for helping me get to where I needed to go. I wouldn't have witnessed the countless miracles that only occur when you are purely surrendered in faith walking into the unknown. I wouldn't be writing this story right now…

Beautiful soul, thank you for reading my story. Many blessings on your journey to healing, wholeness and love.

Throw your dreams into space like a kite, and you do not know what it will bring back, a new life, a new friend, a new love, a new country."

— **Anaïs Nin**

Hayley Scott

hayleyscott.com.au

The Scott's — who are we? My name is Hayley Scott, I'm thirty-five and married to Marty with one daughter Lily (who, by all accounts, is very smart, with a whole lot of sass). I grew up in the UK with my Mum and Dad and older sister. At eighteen years old, I came to Australia on a one year working holiday. I spent the next three years between Australia and the UK before emigrating in 2003 and I haven't looked back. Fortunately for me, my Mum and Dad were very supportive, basically telling me I would be mad if I didn't stay in Australia. And of course, they were right. I absolutely love living here and couldn't think of anywhere else I'd rather be.

I spent almost a decade working in the university sector, leading teams in the student service centre environment. I worked with some amazing people; friends who became like my own Aussie family, helping me to quickly settle and enjoy my new life down under. Living away from my family has been tough at times, none more so than in 2005 when I lost my Dad at the age of 49. Losing a parent is devastating. Losing a parent so young is cruel. Losing a parent while living on the other side of the world, well there aren't really many words to describe it. I miss my Dad terribly and admire my Mum's strength and resilience.

In 2007 I met my now husband Marty (in a very classy establishment, I might add!) Marty and I lived in the city together for a while, before buying a block in his hometown of Waroona (100k's south of Perth). In 2011 we built and moved into our home. We were in the throes of planning our wedding and I started a new job as a HR consultant in local government — nothing like a few projects on the go all at the same time! But we survived, and in 2012 were married at the perfect venue in Ferguson Valley. In March 2013 we welcomed our daughter, Lily Robyn Scott, into the world and needless to say, our lives changed forever! Lily is now four years old and is almost at the end of her first year at Kindy. We like to think she's a pretty cool kid, with tons of personality (a little bit cheeky) but ever so kind. Does she drive us up the wall at times? Of course! She's a curious four-year-old with approximately 426 questions per day and the attention span of 3.4 seconds. We are certainly kept on our toes and life for us is always busy. Marty is an electrical supervisor who works hard (and plays hard!) I have to remind him that we are not the young twenty-five-year-olds we once were! Marty recently returned to footy, coaching the local reserves team. Lily and I enjoy supporting Marty and the footy boys. It's a big commitment but seeing how much Lily loves the environment and watching Marty thrive as coach, makes it all worth it.

At Christmas 2014 I received some pretty shitty news: I was diagnosed with multiple sclerosis (MS). It was most certainly a life changing event and in the immediate days and weeks that followed, I was consumed by my new diagnosis. But, I decided very early on that I would not be beaten by MS. I made some significant changes to my lifestyle, some of which were long overdue! I took a holistic approach to my wellbeing, changing the way I ate and drank, getting back in to exercise and enrolling in further study to nourish my mind. Having not exercised for some time, I set myself a fitness goal: to run 12k in the annual City to Surf. My first efforts on the treadmill were neither pretty, nor epic. I think I ran a total of 1.24 minutes, but I persisted and completed my goal that first year. I have entered the City to Surf each year since and this year completed my first half marathon. Go me! Changing my diet has probably been the hardest part of my MS journey. I have always had a terrible diet (think: meat, carbs, sweet treats, coke, no fruit or vegetables or water). Slowly but surely, I introduced more of the things I should be eating and removed many of the things I shouldn't!

It's a no brainer that with a better diet and some regular exercise, I feel better. In fact, I have more energy than ever before.

I have always enjoyed learning and investing in my personal development, and in 2015 I discovered a new passion. I came across a course of study that I couldn't pass up – Positive Psychology! What is it, I hear you ask? In a nut shell it is the scientific study of what makes humans flourish and live meaningful lives. I spent six days of intense learning and immediately fell in love with this science. I will never forget speaking to the course facilitator during those early days and saying to her, "I don't know how I will ever do this justice" (meaning: how will I describe positive psychology to others who have had no experience with it?) Her very sound advice to me was, "Just live it yourself". So, that's exactly what I did. I went

on to complete my studies and began implementing many
of the things I had learnt into my own life.

My business – the what and the how
If you ask my friend and mentor D, she will probably tell
you we have had the discussion about me doing
'something' for at least six years! It has certainly not been
an overnight decision or opportunity that has enabled me
to do this. So, what am I doing and why now? I'll start with
the what. Right now, I am very much in start-up mode,
launching www.hayleyscott.com.au. My business offers
business coaching and MC services. The reason I finally
decided to bite the bullet? Well, there are two main
reasons, really. Firstly, I started to get some pretty cool
opportunities coming my way, in the speaking space as
well as an opportunity to write a story to be published in
a book. I realised that I could potentially be passing up
other opportunities if I didn't have somewhere for people
to go to find me and what I do. The second reason, while
not so tangible, is that it feels right. Sounds 'woo-woo' I
know, but as I began to really think about what I wanted
hayleyscott.com.au to be, I started to gain some
momentum and decided to just go for it. As I said, this
has been a process over six or so years; there has been
many a note book filled, and stacks of butcher's paper
drawn on with ideas about my own business.

Over the years I have done many things, sometimes
because I enjoyed it, other times because I really wanted
to learn about a particular topic. It has included reading
books, listening to podcasts, attending business seminars,
asking questions of people in business, visiting the small
business centre, and doing online webinars. All of these
things have added to my skills and knowledge, and I know
I will draw on them at different times. I also followed a
couple of processes to help me focus on what I wanted to

do. The processes included writing out 'a day in the life of me'- this is that 'dream space' stuff where you think about your ideal day. What does it look like? Where are you? What does work look like? How are you working (in an office or from home, or at the beach)? etc. etc. Just prior to me commencing my coaching qualifications, I also wrote out a list of intentions; things I wanted to happen over a certain period of time.

The incredibly talented Jack Delosa said, "When the voice inside your head is louder that the voices outside of your head, you have begun to master your life." I'd love to insert the hands up emoji right now, because finally, things started to make sense! The voice inside my head was pretty strong, but also very consistent. I would wake up most mornings and go straight to my notebook (which by now, I carried everywhere with me). Right now, I am really defining what my coaching services will look like, understanding who my target market is and the types of packages I will offer. My values have always been pretty clear to me, so being able to hone in on these for my business was an exciting part of the start-up process.

Essentially, I will be bringing together a few key elements:

- My studies and accreditations, which include: a postgraduate degree in Business Leadership and Management, a Diploma of Positive Psychology and Wellbeing, and I'm currently undertaking my qualifications in Professional Coaching and Neuro-Linguistic Programming (NLP). I am also an accredited DISC Advanced Practitioner.

- My own experience in various areas: my leadership experience, HR background and customer service skills, my personal journey of managing a life changing medical condition and implementing many positive changes. Not forgetting of course, being a mum as well.

- And finally, my passion and huge desire to help make a difference in the lives of female, emerging leaders. There's nothing I want more than to work with women in business and empower them to dream and achieve big.

The other aspect of my business is the MC services. I really like being on the stage. I'm pretty sure I should have enrolled to do musical theatre, but I can't really sing, so MC'ing was the next best thing! In 2016 I was coached by a truly remarkable and selfless person, Suzanne. I need to tell you the story of how Suzanne and I met, because it makes me smile when I think about how these things in life occur. In mid-2016 I was researching various coaching qualifications and I read an article via LinkedIn (not actually about coaching; I think it was a leadership article), but I liked what I read, so I looked up the author. It was Suzanne. I connected with her via LinkedIn and moments later, she sent me a message. "Hi Hayley, lovely to connect with you, have a great rest of the week." I was quite surprised to receive a message, literally just saying "Hi" without trying to sell me anything! So, I decided to reply and ask Suzanne about her coaching qualifications. Once again, she replied within minutes, giving me some really useful information. About a week later, I went to a book launch and presentation, there were some refreshments and networking prior to the presentation and in walked Suzanne. She spotted me and said, "I'm not sure why we know each other but I recognise your face". I then explained that we had sent a few messages to each other via LinkedIn about coaching qualifications. She remembered, and we chatted until the book presentation began. It turned out that we are both from the UK and lived about twenty minutes from each other in the same county and had been in Australia about the same length of time. It kind of blew my mind!

I messaged Suzanne a short time later, asking if we could catch up, which of course, being the super kind and generous person that she is, agreed. It wasn't long after that, that Suzanne sent out a message to her networks explaining that she would like to coach others in how to MC at events. She asked for people to contact her if they were interested. When I first saw the message, I was keen, then that little bit of doubt crept into my thoughts, but before I knew it I had put my name forward. Suzanne coached a group of us in all the things we needed to know about being an MC. I felt incredibly lucky to be learning new skills, as well as meeting other like-minded women. At the end of the program all our names were going to go into a hat and whoever's name was drawn out would be fortunate enough to MC an event that Suzanne had been contracted for (with permission from the event organisers, of course). During the week leading up to the final coaching session, I experienced more self-doubt with some self-sabotage thrown in. I was on the verge of messaging Suzanne to explain that I didn't feel it was fair to put my name in the hat as I wasn't ready to take on such a task if my name was pulled out. There were others in the group that I felt were more deserving, more ready and better than me. And then it was almost like someone smacked me around the head. I thought to myself, *I have literally been given an amazing opportunity to learn and develop new skills and here I am potentially passing up another opportunity to practice what I've learned.* I mean, what was I thinking? I never sent the message, but I knew with 100% certainty that it was my name that would be drawn out. And sure enough, it was. Suzanne and I continued to work together as she coached me through the upcoming event. It was going to be a great experience to put my learnings in to practice, but equally overwhelming at the prospect of standing on stage in front of hundreds of people. I MC'd the event and thoroughly enjoyed it. I also received some pretty positive feedback, particularly as it was my first event. From that moment onwards, I knew I wanted to continue speaking and started thinking about other events I could do. Since then, I have MC'd at various events, from conferences to charity events. That's how coaching and MC'ing came about, and my business is my new baby.

My strategies
Over the course of the last few months (okay, realistically, years!) I have grappled with so many emotions and feelings, particularly around starting a business. Some days I am akin to the energizer bunny (quite annoying, I have been told) and other days I wonder what the f*ck I'm doing. Quite literally. I am pleased I get to share the ups and downs with you, but more importantly, what I have done (or am doing) to overcome the challenges to enable me to forge ahead.

Strategy number 1: Connection

One of my core values is connection. Like Brené Brown, I too believe that connection is why we are here. I know for me, without support from people around me, this business shenanigans would be a whole lot harder. Let me take you back to 2015 when I became a member of a networking organisation called Business Chicks. (If you haven't heard of them, look them up now!) A friend of mine was a member and had recently been on a three-day retreat with a small group of other members. She told me about her experience and I knew I had to look into this organisation. I signed up to become a premium member instantly. I was drawn to everything about them and wondered how I had not come across them before. After attending my first event as a member, I sent the CEO a message to tell her how impressed I was. The event was second to none and the events team were incredible. I literally just wanted to tell her 'thank you'. What happened next? The CEO replied of course! From then on, I have been a huge supporter of all that Business Chicks does. The events and speakers are always first class, but more than that, the support you get from the business chicks team and other business chicks members is quite remarkable. In 2016 I received a phone call from the events team asking me if I could host their upcoming networking event in Perth.

They said I could think about it and get back to them, but this time there was no hesitation — I said yes immediately, so grateful to be given the opportunity.

I will shortly be heading to the Business Chicks annual conference for the second year running and the timing is perfect. I know that not only will I learn from the stellar line-up of presenters, but it is also an opportunity for me to connect face-to-face with other members. I'm hoping to connect with people who have been on a similar path as me and gain some insight into what they've done.

You've already heard me talk about D and Suzanne, my mentors. They've been in my life for varying periods of time and while they are both in the leadership coaching space, I gain something different from each of them. I feel exceptionally lucky to have met them and am so grateful for their time and sound advice, be it via text or face-to-face over coffee.

Of course, my hubby Marty needs a mention here too. I get to do all the things I enjoy and put my efforts into creating my business because he supports what I'm doing, but more importantly, he gets my 'why'. I describe Marty as 'the calm to my crazy'. The poor guy gets to observe as I pull out yet another notebook, coloured pens and post it notes and I am often found starting a conversation with the question, "Do you think I'm crazy?" The answer is usually "yes", but it's not because of my latest idea!

My advice: Don't underestimate the power of connection. Some people freak out at the very thought of attending a networking event. I do suggest you give it a go, but that's not the only place you can meet and connect with people. There are lots of groups online; you can find one that resonates with you. Find a mentor or someone who is on the same journey as you. Sometimes you just need to talk to someone who has walked in your shoes, someone who can hold you accountable for things or even someone who just 'gets it' and can share the wins with you (big or small). The reason I shared the story with you about how Suzanne and I met, is because you need to be open to meeting people in all sorts of situations. I'm a believer in things happening for a reason and don't believe that Suzanne and I met by chance.

Strategy 2: Self-Care

Have you heard the phrase lately, 'self-care isn't selfish'? I never really paid much attention to the actual meaning of this, but through managing my MS symptoms and trying to cram so much into my life (work, creating a business, study, family, friends etc.), I soon realised that looking after myself is not only crucial to my health, but also plays a huge part in being able to flourish. So, let's talk self-care!

Let's be honest here for a minute; life isn't always sunshine and rainbows and don't be fooled by the term 'positive psychology'. It does not mean I am positive All. The. Time. Uh uh! Some days I feel like Mary F*ckin Poppins, other days I'm more like Miss Hannigan – I'm sure I'm not alone. So, let's own that shit.

But, there are definitely things I do to help me maintain a sense of balance in my life.

Firstly, every day before I get out of bed, I check in with my position and if I'm curled up I stretch right out and usually put my hands on my hips – wonder woman style (thank you Amy Cuddy!) Then I say something I am grateful for from the previous day. It doesn't need to be huge - some days I'm grateful that the sun was shining, or that Lily put her shoes on the first time I asked her to! This process allows me to start the day with a calm, relaxed and positive frame of mind.

Practicing mindfulness. I am really new to this, having first learnt about mindfulness during my positive psych studies, and then when I went on to do a six-week online course through Monash University. I lean more towards the informal mindfulness practices as opposed to things such as formal meditation, but I have tried various guided meditations, and writing this is a great reminder for me that I should engage with this more often! However, being present each day in a variety of ways is something I try to do, whether it is when I am out walking and noticing the sound of the leaves as they crunch under my feet or looking up and seeing what's going on in the sky…observing rainbows and clouds are great ways to be in the moment. Journaling is another method I use. I love to really connect with my thoughts and capture those on the page. And finally, I breathe. Well, of course I do, right? Otherwise we know the alternative! But, truly connecting with the breath is powerful and can be done anywhere, at any time. I also have a number of quotes, phrases and affirmations that resonate with me. They are captured in many ways for me to draw on them as I need to. Some are written throughout my notebooks, and others are in photo albums on my phone. I also have one in my car that I see every day.

My advice: Engage in activities that light you up and do them often! Dance like no one is watching, exercise (even if it is in your PJs at home), have drinks with the girls, paint, sing, laugh. Whatever makes you feel good, do it! We are more motivated, more engaged and our brains love the dopamine! Practice being grateful every day - it truly is impossible to be stressed and grateful at the same time (isn't that right Emma Isaacs?!) Find ways to practice mindfulness that work for you, become intensely curious and aim to see things as though it's the first time you've experienced it. The benefits are huge, and you'll thank me later.

Strategy 3: Dealing with negative self-talk, Imposter Syndrome and mother's guilt

Hooley Dooley, these are three things that are pretty much guaranteed to leave you like a rabbit in headlights if you're not careful. It is not uncommon for me to find myself in one or all three of these spaces, but I am definitely learning how to manage them as they arise. The self-talk stuff happens a lot for me. It can be, *"no-one will want to read your story"*, or *"you don't know anything about starting a business, you certainly don't know enough to start a business"* or sometimes, *"you're not as good as so-and-so"*. I read a long time ago to 'catch the faulty thinking'. That is, when you hear yourself saying something that is sabotaging you or the 'talk' is having the opposite effect of what you are trying to achieve, notice it. It is the first step in shifting your thinking. I like to challenge the negative thoughts and flip them around. In pretty much everything I do, I'll find a competition, even if it's competing with Lily over who can get dressed the fastest. I do the same thing with the negative thoughts. I compete with them to find more positive ones!

Imposter syndrome is being talked about quite a bit at the moment. It's not just in starting my business that I have experienced it. I had a huge learning curve when I moved into my role as a HR consultant. It was pretty clear that others believed in me, yet I still questioned myself and I wondered when I would be 'found out'; I didn't have the experience that others did and in general felt like I was doing a disservice to my business partners, even though the feedback was completely the opposite! And of course, right now as I start up my business some days I am paralysed by it, feeling like a complete fraud. When it happens, I usually take a break from what I'm doing. I acknowledge the thoughts and feelings and explore whether there is any truth in them.

Two words here that absolutely do not serve us well, yet so many of us experience it and possibly more than we want to admit: *mother's guilt*. I'm definitely still learning how to deal with this and will share a very recent example of how I had an internal meltdown.

I had organised to get my professional headshots done as I had a few projects lined up and one very specifically wanted a professional headshot. I knew I needed to get them done anyway, as I am usually asked for a headshot when I do a speaking event. I was working to a pretty tight deadline, so I got in touch with the photographer and we organised a date that would enable her to take the shots and have enough time to edit and get them to me for my deadline. Next, I locked in my fabulous hair and make-up guru. Everything was planned down to the last minute. I would drop Lily at school, shoot down and get my hair and make-up done, then drive an hour to where the photographer's studio was, take the photos, drive home and be back in time to get Lily from school. It's not unusual to have days like this where everything is organised with military precision in order to do the school drop off and pick up. It just makes it a little more challenging because I live in a small country town, so naturally everything I need to do is a drive away.

Then, disaster. The sports carnival was rained off the week before and rescheduled for the same day as my photographs. Fuuuuuuuuck! Now I know this doesn't seem like a big deal, but to me it was. It was Lily's first sports carnival. I had already told her the week before that I would be there, and I was so excited to see her take part (sport was my life when I was a kid, so I was living vicariously through her and secretly hoping she would kick ass on the field – competitive by nature, remember!) There was no way I could let her down, but I also knew I somehow had to get the photos done. I actually felt physically sick. After lots of rearranging, an understanding photographer and a flexible hair and make-up artist, I was able to do both, and it was pure joy to see Lily taking part at the sports carnival. My rational mind knows that I won't be able to go to everything that Lily does, I'm also pretty certain she won't be bothered by that. But right now, there are things I want to be able to do with and for her, so when a conflict comes up, dealing with that is tricky! I have a couple of reminders for myself when I start to feel the guilt. Firstly, I'm quite conscious and deliberate in the things I commit to. I'm also aware that I can't do this alone. The support I have looking after Lily is amazing — and besides, when I start feeling guilty I remind myself that she's probably having way more fun collecting eggs from the chooks with Nanny and Grandpa or eating ice cream at the park and finding rocks with Amanda. It can be hard having to ask for help, but it's also necessary. As they say, it takes a village… And finally, I hope I'm showing Lily what is possible. I want her to grow up knowing that she can create the life she wants and truly enjoy doing it.

My last few words
There are so many phrases or words of advice I have come across - either from reading or listening to podcasts (or let's be honest late-night scrolling on Instagram!) Quite often, it can be conflicting words of advice too; be an expert, you don't need to be an expert, start before you are ready, have a really good plan! I'm not saying don't listen and take these things on board, but they can send you into a spin when trying to make a decision. Essentially, I don't believe there is one right way to starting a business; it works differently for everyone. Of course, do your research and have a 'plan' (I am using this term loosely as I don't believe the plan needs to be a seventy-page, hard core business plan), but more importantly, you need to be congruent with your decision. Trust yourself and listen to your instincts.

If it lights you up — do it! This was a classic saying I learnt while studying positive psychology, but it means so much more than it seems. Our brain really does respond to positive emotions and thus creates optimal functioning.

Try and stay present and enjoy the moments for what they are — the good and the bad. Each little step is a step closer to your goal.

Business is hard. Flying solo is hard. Making the decision to just bloody well go for it was hard for me. But at least taking some small steps means I can see my vision coming to life. A friend recently made a decision about her own career and she said that being able to make the decision herself felt great. And, I couldn't agree more. Making the decision, whatever it might be, is empowering in its own right. It's definitely tough at times, but if you don't give it a go, will you regret that more than if you did?

And finally, make sure you've got a kick-ass support crew! My support comes in so many different forms and I truly couldn't do this without them and just to name a few: my Mum, who is on the other side of the world, but only a FaceTime away. The wonderful Claire who often buys me gifts and writes me notes with some of my favourite, completely cliché sayings — "You got this" is just one example! 'Boss' for listening to me for hours, which he must find exhausting, but he does it so well and has some of the greatest advice (and crap jokes) that keep me sane and grounded. And of course, Marty, who puts up with the 'happy, everything is amazing, life is grand' Hayley, but also the 'grumpy, tired, don't put the cups in the dishwasher that way' Hayley. Lean in to your support crew, they've got your back.

The future of hayleyscott.com.au
As you now know, business for me is completely, brand spanking new. I have some immediate short-term goals, but also some lofty, dream big kinda goals too (that includes buying my first pair of Christian Louboutin's)! As Lily moves into full-time school next year, I hope to

grow both aspects of my business. I'm looking forward to working with many coaching clients, seeing them develop and flourish (that's what lights me up!) as well as hitting the stage as much as possible. I know there will be challenges along the way, new things for me to learn and even more strategies for me to put in place, but "I got this". So, as they say, watch this space!

Hayley

Jennifer Forest

Carrot Patch Content

I run a content development business from Canberra, called Carrot Patch Content. I write media releases, training materials and web copy, and I also create exhibitions. I'm a true digital nomad in that I only need my laptop to work, but you won't find me on the beach or in a kombi van touring the countryside. You will find me at home in my city, where my daughter goes to school and we have our friends and family.

I started my business eight years ago, when my daughter was almost one. I always fully expected to keep on with my career, yet I returned to work after my maternity leave and found the environment terribly unsupportive of working mothers. I was working part-time and working super hard to prove I could keep up with the workload. However, I wasn't receiving support from my manager or the team; some were even undermining my hard work and effort because they didn't want part-timers in the team. So, faced with the unsupportive workplace, plus my very real desire to start my own business, I took the leap and left.

Within a very short term, a former colleague working for a different organisation rang and offered me a contract. So, I took it and from there, I built up different projects and worked for different clients around the country. I now create content for solo entrepreneurs, businesses, government and not-for-profit organisations.

That all sounds great, doesn't it? But, the reality is a whole lot different. In fact, I struggled in the early years of my business with isolation and anxiety. When you go from working in a team environment to working alone, it can be very hard. You have to do *everything* including being your own marketing department and fixing the printer. Today, that's one of the attractions of running my own business in that I get to do everything. I love that there's variety in what I do, and I get to use a range of skills.

I also found that the world of business is very noisy, with lots of conflicting information. There are lots of people keen to sell you their product or service under the pretence that it will improve your sales. You have to be a tough curator of the information out there, though. Every business is different, and what works for one may not work for others. Experience has taught me to be my own strongest advocate, and not to believe everything you see out there.

It has been worth it. My business has given me the best projects I've ever done and opened up a world of opportunities, which I would never have gotten if I had stayed in a 'traditional' job. I now have great work to do, have met and worked with some amazing people, and best of all, I do it on my terms. I have the flexibility to pick up my daughter from school and I also get great projects.

For other mums thinking about starting their own business, I would recommend you work with the skills and experience you have already. It's much easier to build a business if you have the right qualifications and workplace experience behind you. I also would very much recommend that you build up a business aligned with your own personal preferences, strengths and values. In the end, your business is built up around you, so make sure it's what you *want* to do.

Jennifer

My philosophy is that not only are you responsible for your life, but doing the best at this moment puts you in the best place for the next moment."

— **Oprah Winfrey**

Joanne Giles

BROWSE

I love to travel, experience new cultures and taste new and different flavours. I was born in England, but from the age of eighteen months old, grew up in South Africa and feel this is where my passion for travel began. My family moved back to the UK when I was twelve. I am so glad they did, as five years later, at the age of seventeen, I met my future husband.

My career started when I left secondary college at eighteen years old. I worked primarily in administration and secretarial roles in a variety of industries, including a nuclear power station, a book publishing company and also Her Majesty's Prison.

My husband and I married in 2004 and bought our first home together. After years of discussions and debates, we decided to follow our dreams to emigrate to sunnier climates. We wanted to go somewhere with more opportunities, so we decided to sell our first home. With nothing to lose and big dreams, we went for it!

We emigrated to Western Australia in 2006. Amazingly, this is when we found out I was seven weeks pregnant with our first child. We still went for it!

We now have two children, aged ten and six, and also added a golden retriever to our little family. We moved to Sydney in 2010 to follow my husband's career in power generation, and we now live on the central coast of New South Wales. It's paradise here! We live, breathe, eat and play at the beach.

I thrive on change. I am always looking for new ways to improve myself and my business. I started reading about self-improvement and listening to audio programs in 2011 and continue to work on self-improvement daily.

Since having my children and when my youngest was two years old, I chased another of my passions, real estate. I started working in the real estate industry in 2011. I began as a receptionist and then progressed into holiday property management, whilst studying in my spare time for my real estate license. I eventually moved into a real estate sales role. After not a very long time in my 'dream role' I started to become unhappy; I wasn't living the way I wanted to. I wanted to still be everything at home, and be there for my children, however the long hours were coming between my family and I. Family is everything, family comes first for me, always. Something had to give.

I was upset. I had come so far, but it didn't feel right for me. So, I took my energy and focused it elsewhere. *What was I going to do?* This is when I went back to the drawing board. My proudest achievement that stands out the most so far, was starting out in business on my own. I learned that I can do it. I can do anything I put my mind to.

In 2013 I started MADiL Australia. I found MADiL on Instagram and it stands for 'Make A Difference in Life'. I contacted the US brand owner and started the process of importing MADiL interchangeable thongs (flip flops) from California. They are like a charm bracelet for your thongs. I shipped my first load of 2000 pairs to Sydney at the end of 2013. I primarily sold them online. As the name of the brand stated, 'Make A Difference in Life' I found a local children's charity in Sydney and donated 10% of the proceeds from the business to this charity.

In 2015 I hit my first challenge in business. The US based company had decided to close its business permanently. I took MADiL as far as I could do in Australia and tried to sell off all my remaining products. Again, I hit another challenge. *What was I going to do now?* I tried to sell the last stock of thongs at local markets, but there weren't many I could get into because of conflicts of interest with local shops. I hit a road block. This is where I had the idea to create the business I now run. I decided to create my own local market. This way I would solve my problem of selling my remaining products, but also help other small businesses like myself that were also struggling.

So, I put together a business plan and took it to the local council. There were a few hurdles, and I was out of my comfort zone, but I persisted. I put together the paperwork and met numerous times at the council offices. Three months later, I was elated when I got the final go ahead!

My first event, the Terrigal Beach Markets took place in February 2016. The response was huge! We had Scottish pipers that played at the opening of our first market, it was full of stalls, the customers came and shopped, kids had their faces painted, the musicians sang.

This continued month after month, as it does to this day. It's a beautiful location for a local market. The response from stall holders and small businesses wanting to be a part of the market was thriving and I only had so many spaces available, so I decided to open a second outdoor market location on the grounds of a shopping centre to meet demand and then a third event, which is an indoor boutique pop up market within the biggest shopping centre on the central coast.

I was able to help even more small businesses grow, whilst doing what I love and also being there every day for my family.

The name of my business is BROWSE. The purpose of my business is to give small businesses the opportunity to grow their brands and sell their products both online and at our monthly events. The events side of my business includes scouting new event locations, liaising with council and centre management within the shopping centre locations to secure a monthly venue for my events.

My customers are the small business owners who attend my events that are looking to sell their products and grow their brands. My events solve the problem locally; small businesses are able to attend my monthly markets and sell their products on the day, talk to their customers in person and advertise their brands. Once a month, 80+ small businesses have the opportunity to sell their products at my events. I provide value at my events, as it is much cheaper than running their own bricks and mortar store.

I run each one of my markets in harmony and peace. I believe in providing a positive atmosphere at each event I create. Everyone is to be treated with common decency and every question has an answer. Nothing is too big of an ask. Everyone is important. Every aspect of a market runs together seamlessly because everyone comes with a positive energy to get the task done — from organising the musicians on the day, to making sure the walkways are clear. Everything needs to be in place.

I have also created an online market, giving small businesses who attend my events and also those who are unable to attend on the day the opportunity to sell their products online to a wider audience. This is Australia wide, which helps even more small business owners.

In February 2017, we also purchased Coasties Entertainment. We have had local young musicians performing at our monthly events from the very beginning and feel they set the vibe of a market and create the atmosphere. The entertainment side of our business is to give local young buskers the opportunity to perform in front of an audience. I coordinate young buskers' schedules, get them new gigs in the area and also promote both the events and performers via social media.

I feel that my business as a whole gives both local and nationally based small business owners and young entertainers the chance to grow and shine.

Technology has helped my business tremendously. Without it, I wouldn't have a business. Everything is done online to mobilise stall holders each and every month - getting stall holders in place, accepting their payments online and sending them all a market manual with instructions for each market day. Reaching new customers online is a daily process, between scheduling social media posts via Hootsuite and advertising the markets. Hootsuite is a great invention. It saves me so much time during the week and the posts are scheduled at the right times to reach the highest number of customers.

I love the freedom of running my life on my own terms. I get to take my children to school every morning, my husband has been able to join our business full time and get out of the rat race, and I can pick the kids up after school each day and be at every school event. It is the best feeling to be able to be there at every assembly when they are collecting an award or standing up on the stage and giving a speech. When they see me in the audience and wave, it's the best! I feel this is what is defined as success. I am now learning to be prouder of myself and to give myself recognition along the way, as I feel my commitment and persistence to keep on going deserves it. I look at ways to learn from each challenge that is thrown at me.

I am so very proud of the people I work with each month. The talent is amazing; all the creators out there creating, all gathering at these monthly events. Small businesses are now collaborating with each other. From those who launched at one of my markets, that go on and grow each month, to sell out and to the inspirational ones who have grown so much, to go on to open up their very own retail shop front. It's amazing to see where they started from to where they are now, and I feel very honoured to be a part of their journey.

The most significant change I have brought about in business is expanding the local events here on the central coast of NSW and supporting tourism within the area. The impact of the three-monthly events I create gives 80+ small businesses the opportunity to launch and sell their products. The impact this has had on these businesses each month is huge! These small business owners have been able to pay their bills, feed their families, and earn that extra bit of money for sports lessons. This inspires both them and me to continue to grow, and to innovate and expand.

My events encourage both locals and visitors to the area alike to shop local, and to support local small business and expand the area in which we live. This means people are more likely to stay in the area and will encourage others to move here and give back to the small business owner. I love the creation of new things. If I see something that could be improved or a new avenue to grow my business in different ways to the norm, I dive right in. I love what I do as I am helping others - whether it be helping local small businesses to grow and sell in the events I organise or giving the young entertainers a place to perform and the chance to shine.

The world needs more mums in business to create new ways of doing things and to provide others the space and opportunity to shine and grow.

I approach challenges in business as I do in my personal life. If a challenge is thrown at me, there is an opportunity to learn and grow from it for the better. There are challenges every day in business — from the start of running my first ever event, negotiating with local council and answering all their queries, going back and forth out of my comfort zone, and putting together various plans and assessments.

Then, there was my second event. I ran a market in an overspill shopping centre car park, where we had barely any customers shopping. This led to me being offered prime outdoor space within the shopping complex. Without being at the overspill car park that day, I feel we wouldn't have been in the position to showcase what we can do. The centre management were impressed with how we ran the day and admired our business plan, which led to us being offered our next opportunity. This then grew to being offered a prime space *inside* the shopping centre in the centre court position, with even more foot traffic for the small businesses to be seen and to grow. It helps both the small business owner and the customer, as they are all keen to keep things local, support and shop local. Each challenge along the way has forced me to change, to shake things up a little, to innovate and to expand in business.

My family is my support network. My kids keep me motivated each day, and that's why I do what I do. I am also delighted that my husband has now joined the business from a corporate background. So, it's now the two of us in our home office growing our family business together. I also now feel the need to connect with a mentor or business coach and am always looking for new ways to grow my network. I am not quite the social butterfly, so pushing myself to attend networking events is way out of my comfort zone, but every time I do attend an event, I come away pleased that I did attend. There are so many amazing individuals out there creating! You need to get out there and speak with similar minded people. You don't know what you can learn from these opportunities, or what you have to offer someone else.

Our current customer base is locally on the central coast of NSW, however with BROWSE, this will stretch out to a national customer base. We are currently speaking with shopping centres throughout Australia - a couple in Queensland, a number throughout New South Wales, and also a couple in Western Australia. We have the vision to replicate what we have done here locally, across

Australia nationally. I am currently looking to hire my first employee to be involved in the event management side of things, so that I can concentrate on the growth of my business.

What I am doing today with my events has been and will continue to help both individuals and the planet of tomorrow. Through my events, I am encouraging people to shop locally and to support the small business owner, by providing them with events to do so. This in turn brings people to the area and supports tourism and the local economy for future growth. By offering more local events and now, online, more individuals will have even more opportunity to support small businesses on a bigger scale, Australia wide.

The hardest part is to start, to jump in, and not to hold back.

I understand the juggle and the daily routine of being a female entrepreneur. Juggling family life, business, creativity, and looking for other avenues to grow your business while keeping positive along the way can be difficult, but I feel I can reassure mums out there looking at starting that business, that everything will be okay. Keep going. We can all do it. You just need to try and keep your sanity along the way by following your passion and doing what you love.

I would also say to someone starting out that they should be testing the market first. Social media has transformed my events business. Without it, I wouldn't be able to reach as many people. I first started the Terrigal Beach Markets as a Facebook page to gain interest, to see if there was even a need for another market on the central coast. The amount of likes and comments of support reaffirmed my belief that there was definitely a demand for a market in Terrigal.

I want to inspire other young mums and also my own children to follow their passions and remind them that anything is possible. Chase your dreams. Make a to do list and destroy it. I feel we have all already won the lottery by actually being here; by breathing and being alive. The least we can do is live our lives and do what we love. Create a business from your heart's desire and then share your experiences of how you enriched your own life, so that in turn, it will encourage others to do the same, and leave a legacy for the next generation.

In the future, to build on my success and personal brand, I will be by sharing my own story; my why. By sharing my experience in business and life, I would like to inspire others to start that business they have always thought of starting, and to take the leap and believe in themselves. Anything is possible with the technology of today.

Joanne

Kelly McDonald

Garden Babies Fine Fairy Art

When I first submitted an application to be part of this anthology, it was a Friday night, probably around 8.30 because there were no kids bothering me, and I was possibly slightly intoxicated. The application called for stories about mums who work for themselves. I work for myself. I can do this, I thought. And so, I sat down to write. Where to start? What was I thinking? Who cares what I do, or about my little business?

I'd recently been a finalist in the AusMumpreneur awards but due to not being able to fly to Sydney, I wasn't able to accept my nominations, but a lot of people I know were part of it. A lot of them seem to gush with pride, tell of their support, seem well groomed at all times, and didn't talk much about the drinking, nor the finding yourself in your slippers greeting a client at the door with a child hanging off your arm. Maybe I should tell the truth, I thought. Well, my truth anyway.

I work from home, as does my husband. We have an almost eleven-year-old and a four-year-old. Three and a bit years ago I stole the kid's playroom and set up a fairy garden. You see, I'd just had a baby, at forty years old. We had also just upgraded into a beautiful new home, which also came with a beautiful big mortgage. I am a Kinder teacher by trade but had been performing magic and storytelling around Australia (and even a little in Europe) for the past twenty-four years. When we got home from Europe, I went back to Kindy teaching, right up until the day I started puking everywhere and found out I was expecting.

I didn't want to be raising other people's kids while mine was left with some stranger. It just didn't make sense to me to do that. So, I thought about what I could do. I'm a kid's entertainer at heart, and I love giving them the gift of magic, to make everything special for just a moment. I know how to speak to them, and I love seeing their eyes light up in amazement or joy. It makes my heart sing. I was also pretty good at photoshop. I wasn't able to work in Europe, so had started making fairy art using pictures sent to me of children from all over the world. I'd become quite well known for it. I was all self-taught, so my slapdash style was my own.

I loved magick - all kinds - and had studied Wicca and faeries and tales of old for many, many, many years. Through my sleep deprived fuddled mind, a little idea was born. Maybe I could mix it all together. The magic, and the storytelling, my art, the kinder teaching, my love of faeries.

I told hubby my idea but wasn't sure if other people would like it. He wasn't amazed by any means, but he said I may as well try, and see how it goes. There wasn't much I could do until baby was older anyway. I made a background, had it printed, and began to collect my props, (and any random children I could borrow) to get my look together. It worked. People liked it. The first year in, I won the AusMumpreneur award for service. I took my mum to the awards, and I was so glad that I did! She glowed with pride. Mum is my biggest supporter. From buying props, to replacing broken lenses, she is there every step of the way.

All sounding pretty good hey? *swishes hair, pops hand on hips, applaud me, applaud me! Well, keep reading.

In my house, my husband has the 'real' job. This little venture of mine brings in a little money, but also takes me out of the twenty-four-hour cleaning role, except it's only me who does it. I'm the wife. It is my job. I've heard there are new rules about this 'his and hers' job sharing thing… but I don't know where you are meant to apply for one of those husbands. Most of my friends didn't get that memo either.

I mentioned I work from home, yes? My clients come here. Sometimes they need a bathroom. I have some of those… but I also have those kids remember. One is a boy and pees on the floor constantly and the other's four, so she doesn't flush a lot and will sometimes leave surprises. I need to make sure that they are clean and okay before the clients arrive at 10am. I don't always make it and feel irk when they ask, "Can we just borrow the loo?"

I do the school runs. And the kinder runs (what the hell is wrong with these kinder session times! Who made those up?) ….and the shopping, and the bed times, and the bathing, and the housework. I can't get a housekeeper, because I don't have a 'real' job. It's my job to be the wife and mum, and take care of the kids and all, but I also need to make *** dollars a week, please.

> Come 5.01, or sometimes 4.35, I have a wine in hand most nights. Well, not on the two low cal day. The washing sits on the couch. I do that at night, hang it out when I can. Sometimes it is there for a few days.

One day on his lunch break, (he gets one of those - he takes the dog for a walk and such) hubby said, "Suns out, shouldn't you get that washing out to dry?" Yes, he still lives... it was probably a 4.35 wine night that night. No, I don't have the best support from my husband. That's okay! He doesn't see my bigger picture. He doesn't understand my need to do something that isn't mum or wife related, and who the hell grows up thinking, "I just want to clean a house all day, yay!" Not me.

I'm not meaning to sound angry or anything like that. He has old fashioned values; he has the 'real' job. But, I can't not do my best and I can't not be creative, and oh my lord, I hate housecleaning, but I have to do it because (for now) that is the way it is! But, I have my outlet. My Garden Babies.

I opened a childcare business at sixteen years old, then a kinder at twenty-one. My fairy business at twenty-three (yes, I've been a fairy more than half my life) and my photography business at forty. It is my baby and I adore watching it grow. I love to succeed, and I love to write. I love to create, and even though some days it's really, really hard to get any work done around my mum and wife roles, I still scratch it out and cope the best I can.

I answer the door in slippers. I excuse myself when I'm upstairs working, and my kids somehow lock themselves in the cupboard downstairs. I get up early to edit. I go to sleep dreaming of what I have to edit the next day, how many edits to get through, what time my client is coming, and oh shite, did the kid need a costume for that school thing tomorrow? That's the reality. If I don't get it done, it just doesn't. Somehow, I stay mostly on top. I ignore the grumbles of the man of the house as best I can. I try to make an effort to go and see a friend, even if just for a cuppa once a fortnight or so. I try to turn off the PC work when the kids get home from school. I try.

It has been four years and each year my little business grows and grows. I've been awarded by my peers and my clients. Every session gets me rewarded (emotionally, creatively and monetary). I have repeat clients, and awesome followers, and just this week I found out I got a lease on a little shop, so I can move out of the house and have a little space for my own fairy land. I'm glad it was hubby's idea to get a studio (finally). I mean, why pay for a space when I have it for free here at home and I can do house stuff around my work? The client's kids who were here one day eating cereal at my table with my kids kind of helped that idea along, hehe.

So now, I'm going to have room to expand and a little room to breathe. I can provide more options to bring in more cash flow and offer my clients more value and magic for their dollars. Of course, that means I may have to do the housework at night. I know this, but maybe I will get a cleaner after all. Now that I'll have a 'real' job.

It's worth it. This little business is a piece of my heart. It gives to me and allows me to give back.

You've got to follow your heart. You have to dream big. You must have a place for you - not the mum or wife part

- the *inside* part of you. Don't let anyone say no, you can't.

I still have a long way to go to be stronger, and to take my journey further, but it's mapped out...on a trail of fairy dust.

So, the business end of things. What do you do if you have an idea?

1. Write it down. Plan it out on paper. What do you need to start? Can you do it small scale first? Maybe market it as a hobby to begin with (you can earn a fair whack without paying tax if it's a hobby)
2. Where are your peeps? Your clients? Where do they hang out? Think of ideas of how you can get your product or service to them. You do not have to pay high end marketing and advertising.
3. Can your product or service help another business or organisation? Ask them.
4. Use Facebook! Don't like Facebook? I don't care, use it! It is free. You don't have to run ads. I use Facebook every day. I make contact with my clients every day. I ask them questions. I allow them to be part of my journey (you have no idea how your followers want you to succeed and be amazing! I have made so many new friends and get so much support from my clients). So, use Facebook (and Instagram and whatever else works for you).
5. Give back where you can. I give a lot of my work to kids battling cancer and other terrible things. It's my way of giving back.
6. Use vouchers. Entice them in but be wary as free often means people don't respect it, so think of ways to entice, but still make it valuable to them.

(the only freebies I give are to sick kids. I give $$$$$ away in vouchers, but just for a portion of what I offer, not the whole shebang).
7. Value yourself and your time. It's a hard one. I know my fees are well below anyone else who does anything similar to me and I am working on my self-worth (and prices).
8. Find a mentor for the hard bits.
9. Delegate the harder bits to someone else. Sometimes paying someone else to do something you despise takes the burden from your shoulders and gives you time to get the work done you need to.
10. Believe in yourself. Nod and grin to the naysayers, and do it anyway, but do it well!

There's also all the planning stuff. What do you need from your council's point of view? Then, there is your insurance, your policies, your contracts and legal obligations. Get legal advice and talk to a good accountant. Such as, did you know if you hire staff and they earn more than $450 a week you also must pay super?

Finally, lay down a carpet of glitter (or rose petals if you prefer) and give yourself pats on the back, a day off occasionally, and enjoy bringing your business to fruition. For me, it is a mark of who I am. Do it, do it well, and cover it in glitter!

I always did something I was a little not ready to do. I think that's how you grow. When there's that moment of 'Wow, I'm not really sure I can do this,' and you push through those moments, that's when you have a breakthrough.

— **Marissa Mayer, former CEO of Yahoo**

Natalee Anderson

Fat Burning Women

When does a business actually begin? When you register with the tax office, or pick a name? Is it when you make the decision to start, or maybe when you get that very first spark of an idea? Or, is it when you find something you are truly, madly, deeply passionate about? Perhaps it's simply that you have a really big problem, and there just is no answer; so, you create one. And then, to create the answer for yourself but not share it with the world, could be considered selfish... Well, that, and finding a solution to such a big problem is actually so empowering; and exciting; and ignites a fire so deep in the heart that you will weather any rejection, sleepless night, tears or sacrifice, just so you can share it with the world.

And that is how it started for me. A very big problem. I didn't plan to be in business, I just wanted the simple life; to climb the corporate ladder and be the very best and most successful woman ever, so I could make my dad proud. My version of that was a high paying job with a swanky job title, a few awards, a house, a couple of smart investments, nice cars, two kids, and probably playing netball or running at a professional level, oh and couple more sports awards too. An overachiever. An under-believer. Driven by ego and a lack of self-love. Highly motivated, but never good enough. And oblivious to any other reality.

Until my very big problem in June 2010.

To be honest, the problem started well before 2010, but it was in 2010 I became aware, and like any area of life that requires change, you can't take responsibility until you are aware. So, in June 2010 I flew back to New Zealand to meet my precious new nephew and my very big problem.

I had never been a big fan of the cold, but this year was different. I had been accustomed to pain for numerous years but limited to my perception at the time; I had thought the pain and stiffness was from exercise. In June 2010 however, I wasn't exercising, but the pain and stiffness started to escalate. First, I couldn't bend my leg, and then I couldn't stand up straight or walk properly. Then, I couldn't sleep without waking in incredible agony and even to hold a pot with my hands felt impossible. The pain and stiffness slowly took over my body and left me confused, scared and feeling powerless.

On returning to Australia I was diagnosed with an incurable and degenerative auto-immune arthritis. The prognosis: fusion of the spine and a warning of a life in a wheelchair – translation in my eyes - 'end of my life'. For someone who competed nationally in four sports, to not be able to walk, run or jump equaled not good enough, no value, worthless. And so, my life came crashing down.

I lay in bed for sometimes sixteen hours a day, exhausted, tossing and turning and trying to ease the pain. My brain became consumed, and everything I thought of doing was burdened by the fear of the pain. I was scared to drive, to go to the shops, to see friends, to sit in a meeting at work, to stand, to walk, to sit, or lie down. I was scared. All I could think about was pain and trying to avoid it. 24/7.

And so, I cried.

I cried most days and through the night, walking around with tears in my eyes, unable to see anything else. But, life has a funny way of using painful twists and turns to direct us to our fate, if we are willing to surrender to it. So, with my version of a 'fatal' diagnoses, a face full of tears and a caramel latte in a paper coffee cup warming my aching hands, I picked up a magazine with a girl on the front. A girl with an *actual* fatal diagnosis. She had a terminal cancer and was healing her body with holistic therapies, after conventional medicine failed her. This gorgeous soul, dressed in a cabbage leaf dress, thriving with cancer, is enough to squash any excuse, ever.

With renewed hope and curiosity, I set off on a path of holistic health, searching for the answers of a fulfilled life with no pain and a healthy, thriving body. Little did I know this pivotal moment was to shape the platform of our business, Fat Burning Women - to overcome any pain, problem, struggle or resistance is the gateway to free others from their pain.

So, like many enthusiastic lost souls on a health and wellness journey, I googled the shit out of my problem. The conventional medical system had given up on me, my condition was to worsen over time, and I was only given medication to slow the progress. Lucky for many of us, information is readily available and there is no shortage of healing protocols that have worked for a lot of people. I tried a vegan diet, I went paleo, I did 'GAPS' healing protocol and I even tried Gerson. I threw out all my toxic cleaning products, ate clay and dirt, and even practiced regular enemas. I discarded anything in my cupboard that did not align with 'extreme' healing. My frugal fiancé at the time stood back horrified.

While I threw myself wholeheartedly into this new world of holistic health, I found myself angry at anything and anyone that wasn't pure. I would arrogantly preach my new-found love and why everyone should convert to whole living, like, right now. Many people lapped up the knowledge I shared and fed my ego, but deep down I was still living in fear. My condition hadn't improved, and I was uncertain of my future. Driven by my fear and not knowing if my pelvis would fuse, we decided to start having kids earlier than planned; a sure sign I did not believe I could heal my condition. The moment my fiancé turned husband looked at me, we fell pregnant; we certainly have been blessed with fertility, which I am forever grateful for.

Becoming a mum was not what I expected it to be.

I never held my daughter when she was born, ICU was her mother for the first few weeks. This trauma was only the start of a tumultuous relationship where I was miserable the first few years of her life. It seemed everyone around me was able to follow the rule book, to make parenthood work. Me, I ended up with an emotionally volatile three-year-old that still didn't sleep through the night and taking a heavy dose of antidepressants just to survive each day. Three years of a child's crying and sleep deprivation can damage an already damaged woman.

I was able to find some refuge in my work. Being on maternity leave allowed me some freedom to dip my toes into the ocean of business. I lovingly shared my journey of holistic health and parenthood - without any real idea of what I was doing, but certainly enjoying the distraction. And then, with a blog and a short sugar detox program, I guess I had the makings of my first business. To market and sell myself however was a whole other story!

I did some coaching with friends for free and sold the program for I think, $7. I tried to set up paid advertising on my blog, but it turns out I didn't have enough traffic for anyone to care. My precious ego that lead to all my previous success, started to become my biggest weakness. I desperately held onto people's opinions, and willingly went on the emotional rollercoaster ride, crashing each time I was rejected. This attachment to the outcome is not sustainable or conducive to growth. But, the fear of being rejected kept me playing it small. Low risk, low vulnerability, low results. I shared my healing knowledge as I learnt it, more regurgitation style than anything pretty. But surprisingly, I did have some loyal followers who are still engaged and loyal to this day. For some strange reason, I didn't become a millionaire, despite all my knowledge and passion to change the world.

And then, my maternity leave was up. At this stage I had not quite jumped into a real entrepreneur mindset; the concept of not going back to work had not even crossed my mind. On reflection, this represented my low commitment to myself, my business and my purpose. I had a fallback plan and I went straight back to it – that, and I couldn't stand to be at home with my daughter full time anymore.

The return to work honestly, was shit. I had been the highest performing manager for about five years prior. I spent twelve months away and on returning to the building, felt insignificant. When I left my managers office, I felt like she had taken a big dump on my ego and

I could feel a big lump in my throat as I tried to swallow my pride. I was required to go back full time to retain my job, which wasn't physically possible. My daughter wouldn't take a bottle and just cried, like all day, she was boob obsessed and had attachment issues. And, I am not exaggerating. One of her first child care teachers expelled her. She lasted 1.5 days. Despite the carer's '12 years' experience', she couldn't handle the crying. Children are so misunderstood; especially those with high needs. But, I guess in fairness, I think I was going back to work just to avoid the crying too.

So, unable to be away from my daughter five days a week, I went to part time. I dropped my role in management and spent my time as a customer service consultant. My fragile ego took another massive hit and I lost all confidence in myself. Over a few months, I sunk into a deep, worthless heap, not seeing the beauty already inside of me. As it has in the past though, my arrogance and obsession with being the best drove me to work my way back up to management, even in a part time role. And then, I decided to tempt fate with baby number two.

After the traumatic birth number one, birth number two was about as magical as, I suppose, birth can be? We gave birth at home in the shower to my calm little boy - raw, vulnerable and empowered. I was free to hold him for an hour, the heavenly gift of touch and I got lost in time and space. After the hour was up, he left the room while I had my stiches and was brought back to reality. But then, I walked out into the lounge.

There on the couch was my gorgeous three-year-old girl, holding her sparkling new brother. All I could see was a deep pride and love in her eyes. A bond that would never break.

So, this was my chance. Maternity leave number two. Twelve months to create a rocking business with financial freedom, so I wouldn't need to go back to work. With my magical second child, so peaceful and calm, I soaked up all the goodness of being a mum of a new born for sixteen weeks before I got itchy feet and wanted to start 'the business' again. As fate would have it, I crossed paths with a coach who helped other coaches build an online business. And so, on a whim, I decided it was now or never and invested a huge chunk of our money in him, along with 100% faith.

I was up till late at night learning about 'my why', niches, sales, marketing, funnels, branding, goals, software, business and program structures, plus so much more - while still getting up at 2am to feed my delightful baby. Each sleep break he took during the day I was learning, absorbing, and putting into practice everything I'd learnt. I was a diligent student to my new master. It was exhausting, but I so loved learning, following a blueprint and trusting the process, I felt like I had wasted so much time fluffing around first time around.

When I followed the process laid out before me, leads trickled in and I practiced selling my program over the phone. I was excited, but still had little confidence and was actually pretty unclear on what I was offering and the outcomes my clients would get. This came across in my calls and most people baulked at the price. But I kept persevering, refining my funnel and getting better on my calls. I ran a couple of Facebook '7 Day Challenges' with awesome feedback, but still, no one wanted to pay me money for the awesome 'information' I was sharing.

My health along this process was progressing 'good enough', but I was still a tired mum who spent most of my time lying down with the kids climbing all over me. Our early family videos and photos, I am often still in my PJs, lying down or even in bed. I had bought into the idea this was okay. I am a mum of a baby. But, it's not.

I say it's not okay, not to offend anyone's belief of being kind and non-judgmental to mums. I am saying 'It's not okay' because my body wasn't thriving, and it was capable of so much more. I am saying 'it's not okay' because I bought into the societal idea that it was okay. When I let go of that belief, that I should be tired, or have baby brain, I opened up the possibility to be better.

And then, I got a coach to help me do so.

I had a coach to help me with my business and then got a coach to help me with my health. It makes sense, right? If you want to save time researching, practicing and failing numerous time, if you want to fill in all the missing pieces and get results in twelve weeks instead of six years, then you pay the money and get a coach. So, I did.

My coach had shared a lot of the information I already knew, but he put it together in a nice sequential order. We made 20% changes, for 80% of the results. That's what coaches do. They see the problem and they fix it. They see your blind spot and they show it to you. Sometimes in a brutally honest way. The small changes that we made allowed my hormone insulin to get low enough for me to tap into my fat stores. I was able to start metabolising fat full time instead of glucose. The high amount of money invested meant that I was totally committed and stuck to the plan wholeheartedly for at least twelve weeks to actually get results. And, the results were nothing short of amazing. I had a vibrant energy that lasted all day, my brain fog cleared, and I started remembering more. I felt like I was buzzing and joyous all the time, and the sleep that I did have felt restful and restorative.

I had so much energy that I started running, but I never felt tired or sore. I ran and ran and ran and never felt the need to stop. My kilometres started creeping up and before I knew it, I had run half a marathon just in training. I decided to run a full 42km marathon, despite having never run over 10km before, due to the limitations of my body. I honestly felt like superwoman, and limitless. I chose to keep pushing and pushing. And then, the day after my marathon, I was painless. No pain whatsoever in my body. As far as I was concerned, this was impossible. What I had created in my body was beyond my wildest dreams, but it also didn't make sense. So, I sought out a professor in South Africa who did a coaching course on this method. I needed to understand what had just happened in my body and, so I started my studies of fat metabolism.

One of my business coach's mottos is 'be a progressionist, not a perfectionist' and one of his favourite quotes this year seems to be 'action precedes clarity'. So, before I even finished my studies, I started marketing and selling the program I was going to build. The program would not only balance hormones to reset the metabolism, but also address all the barriers to sustainable results; like self-sabotage, emotional eating, motivation, stress, other key hormones, busyness, self-esteem, sleep and even how to put yourself first or say no. If a 'very big problem' was the beginnings of my business, the business just went from a fetus to a new born baby. Fat Burning Women was born.

Like most of my experience in my journey so far, 'leads' trickled in slowly. I knew I was building an amazing life changing product - it had changed my life - but now to convince the whole wide world that they should trust me to help them.

Well, it seems fate was about to give me the biggest hurry up of my life.

One week before Christmas, my husband was hearing rumours around his office that the company was going under. Within two days of those rumours, the doors closed. News crews were hovering hungrily at the entrance, interviewing staff as they attempted to open the locked doors. No one knew for sure what was happening, but one thing was for certain; there was no work that day. Communication was non-existent from there on out, bits and pieces of the story were pulled together to paint a very bleak picture that there would be no job and no pay, a week out from Christmas.

It was a tough Christmas to endure, with no certainty and minimal opportunity. At every chance, my husband would apply for work, with the only available options two hours' drive away in Brisbane. With a young family, four hours of travel each day certainly wasn't ideal. It would also mean the end of Fat Burning Women, and our metabolic reset program. The worst part was though, even those job opportunities that were available in Brisbane were not successful. Each glimmer of hope kept fading.

But then, I started seeing numbers repeating, everywhere. I looked them up. I had never been a spiritual person. Religious yes, spiritual, not at all. But these numbers, according to google, were my angels talking to me. I couldn't help but take comfort in the messages and I can honestly say, there were times when the only thing that kept me going was their promise; I was on the right track, keep forging ahead faithfully. So, I did.

Then there was a moment when I crossed paths with a Facebook ad — simple, a little primitive even - but it had photos of testimonials. Emails from clients asking to have their ads turned off as they had too many leads. Too many leads? Well, that's definitely a problem I want to have. I think that's a problem everyone wants to have, right? A short conversation later and I was pitching to my husband, the dream. We would have way too many leads for my program, we would have hundreds of clients and he would not have to go back to work. He could be a stay at home dad rather than driving four hours round trip to work each day. Sounds perfect, doesn't it?

It was from that moment we looked at life differently.

We decided first, that we were committed to our dream lifestyle, and then second, to figure out how. Most people try to figure out how to create the dream before taking action and living it. They spend most of their lives planning and never actually get there. They may do their business part time while working a job until they have enough time, money or confidence to leave, but then they never do. Or maybe they wait until they have finished their studies, but then they take more courses to feel more qualified, confident or sure. As my coach says, 'action precedes clarity', so I took action before knowing how it would all work out.

We gambled the last of our money on this marketing company to deliver leads. I had to produce video content, blogs and video testimonials for them to use in the Facebook funnel. And as the leads came in, I had to very quickly build my program.

See, everyone has a 'push' and 'pull' motivation, the carrot and the stick. The pain of where you are now 'pushes' you forward into action toward the goal and the vision of your dream outcome 'pulls' you forward. To increase motivation, you can either spend time loading up the consequence of where you are now, making the pain so great you have no choice to move forward or, spend time immersed in your goals and dream so it becomes a real, living organism. Or, both. When you spend all of your money on an investment, trusting that it will work, you have no choice but to be motivated and take action, every single moment. I had created the biggest push motivation of my life, the consequence of not succeeding meant we had no money. No money meant no food for my family, no mortgage, so no roof over my family's head. I nearly threw up.

That is fear. That is action preceding clarity.

So, with no money and living on a prayer, we actually moved out of our house temporarily, so we could pay the mortgage. Temporarily turned into about three months while we worked our butts off to create regular cash flow. We started getting about a hundred new inquiries a week for our 12 Week Metabolic Reset Program and I sold people over the phone with a $1200 promise. I quickly learnt that no one wants a 12 Week Metabolic Reset Program, well, no one really wants any product or service, what people really want is results, an outcome. So, with previous success and testimonials, I made promises to my new clients with confidence and certainty. This opened up a regular influx of new clients into the business.

The flow was steady and fast, and as I spent so much time in the front end, sharing our message and bringing in new clients, I struggled to keep up with servicing our existing customers. I had built an amazing program that was self-sufficient and delivered life changing results for those people that followed it, but I didn't account for one thing — the human factor. Our program relied on self-motivation from clients, that is how I had got results from my coach, so I kind of expected everyone to be like me. Disciplined, obsessive, stubborn and relentless. Probably a good thing not everyone is.

Client retention started dropping, so we brainstormed new ideas to increase customer retention by exceeding customer expectations and pre-empting any drop off. We sent out welcome packs to our clients, unexpectedly, so they would feel the physical value of their electronic purchase. This was a massive hit. Weekly interactive webinars were also introduced. These were designed to publicly celebrate success, share learnings and refocus each week. The focus on progress and proactively addressing concerns and challenges each week lead to an increase in retention up to 100% the very first month. We had very happy customers, sticking to the program and creating a body and life they couldn't even dream up. But, with the new changes and at the same price point, Fat Burning Women barely broke even and I wasn't paying myself a wage either. So, with all the extra value we had added to the program, I felt confident to increase our pricing. Shortly after, sales dropped to zero.

I pondered why this happened, but to this day I am not 100% certain. The price increased from $1200 to $2000 — not a massive jump - so I am not convinced it was this alone. My perception of the price jump was probably of far greater significance. Did I truly believe people would pay $2000 for my health program? The short answer, I think, is no. This mindset affected sales. I did sell a couple of people into our $2000 program initially, but the consequence was my own self-inflicted pressure to make up for the increase in price. If you are not certain of your self-worth, how hard you work is often a reflection of this belief. Me, I was basically on call 24/7 and working stupidly long hours. I did not think I was worth $2k.

See, this is a belief system around self-worth, as well as the problem of focusing on a 'program' or 'product' rather than the 'results' or 'benefit'.

For any woman who is too embarrassed to go to the beach in their bathers with their kids, for anyone who obsessively counts calories, or thinks about how they are going to exercise to burn off every meal, for everyone who looks in the mirror and cries, or can't sleep, or wakes up sore every day, or is so exhausted they can't play with their kids; they would pay $2000 to make that problem go away. These same people would pay $2000 to be free from cravings, to emotionally feel in control, to have the energy to go to the park with their kids or strut their stuff in their bathers at the beach or be confident to be in photos and go out socialising. These women would pay a lot more, for that outcome. And that is value. They are the results. That is sales. Not a program.

So, with a fresh perspective and new staff to support the continuous flow of women seeking to work with Fat Burning Women, we have perfected this product, sales and service. We have new clients that join us each week because they are aware of their problem and know we understand. They also know the results we will get with them. With 100% certainty. They often come to us for weight loss, but leave free from cravings and obsessing over food, no longer controlled by their thoughts and emotions, full of childlike energy, loving the women in the mirror, confident to wear any clothes they wish and loving life. To gift women this new life is truly priceless, and I am so humbled for the opportunity to share this.

To be honest, I'm not sure if this is an inspiring business success story. This is a 'I shit my pants most days' kind of story. This is an 'I moved my kids out of their house to live with the in-laws to keep my business afloat' kind of story. Or maybe, an 'I have no idea what I am doing most of the time, but I take action anyway' kind of story?

I see my business as a moving entity, constantly changing and evolving and it always seems to mirror my own personal evolution. I used to be attached to things being a certain way, patterns being predictable, software doing what I wanted it to, keeping the same friends, money and clients flowing consistently, following business models that are supposed to work. But what I have learnt most is, everything flows exactly as it is meant to, often in ways that you don't think. Getting frustrated is futile and often destructive. Where instead, looking for new opportunities everywhere keeps the excitement alive. Accepting that business comes in seasons, letting go of the old and embracing the new, this allows for peace and flow each and every day.

So, the birth of Fat Burning Women through our transformational 12 Week Metabolic Rest program is now transitioning from a baby to a toddler. Her personality is starting to come through, some parts of her are being left behind as she steps into her own consciousness, her own beauty. What was once a single focus, is now evolving, connecting and weaving a new reality through the river of life. Sometimes she goes off course, but the moment we reconnect to her purpose, her values, her vision, she takes the wheel and drives so effortlessly. On the horizon are images of workshops, events, books, retreats, collaborations and more. And, with each new venture brings with it a different set of challenges.

> **My same beliefs, fears and habits come up, and I continue to (not so elegantly) dance through them. But, I dance.**

I look at my business as a vehicle for becoming the very best version of myself. I would not have developed so exponentially, mentally, spiritually and emotionally without all the impossible challenges I have faced and overcome. I am truly grateful for the opportunity.

I am also so blessed to view life through a new lense. I no longer feel controlled by the 9-5 game. I have been introduced to the bigger picture in life and out of life. There are times that we have no predictable money, but I know I can make money, I never had that freedom before. There are times when it feels so hard, I drown in my own tears and want to give up; but then I have a breakthrough and feel so empowered knowing I am actually capable of more than I ever realised. There are times when my high-needs daughter is about to burst into tears at school and in that moment, I don't have to hurry off to someone else's work. I hold her, she cries. I don't need to say anything, she knows I understand and I am there.

Having that flexibility, the balance of freedom, being in control of my time, success and untapped money potential, is my new map of reality. This is the map of mums in business. It is so much more than just being a mum.

Rochelle Muscat

Pop the Balloon! Children's Parties and Events

For more years than I can remember, an inner voice has persistently told me that I am meant to be 'more than I am'. Frustratingly though, I could never quite put my finger on what that 'something more' was until the day I was made redundant from my successful corporate career. But before I get into that, let me start at the beginning…

My name is Rochelle. I am the owner of Pop the Balloon! Children's Parties & Events and Party Utopia Events — both of which are located on the beautiful NSW Central Coast. I am effectively a 'party PA' to my clients, offering a customised service to create their vision for themed party celebrations for their children and loved ones.

I am also a wife, mother, sister, daughter, friend, business entrepreneur and mentor to young women who (like me) are navigating the joys and challenges of day to day life. I have an amazing husband who is my source of strength and support (and some would say the comic relief in my life!) and together we have been three-times blessed with beautiful children; our son Aidan (aged 6), and daughters Isabella (aged 4) and Arianna (aged 1).

My life thus far has involved a combination of creative and artistic endeavours mixed with the structure and quiet restraint of corporate life.

From the age of four, I began dancing with a local dance academy; finding my feet and confidence on stage and learning to express myself through music and movement. School, tennis lessons, business college and work followed, but until I retired from dance at twenty-four, dancing was my first love and priority. This was largely due to the many and varied opportunities that dance offered. The privilege of teaching children the art of dance, the freedom to express myself artistically through stage performance at local eisteddfods, talent quests and shopping centre shows, as well as one spectacular evening performing in front of royalty at a charity event in Sydney; are a sample of the many highlights of my dancing career to date. I was also most fortunate to be a small part of the teams of creative professionals who promoted the Sydney 2000 Olympic Games at Parliament House and many other venues around NSW in the lead up to that event. I was further privileged to work alongside the (then) Disney Australia and be exposed to, and inspired by, their incredible approach to working with children and family entertainment. My love of dance was equally formed over the years spent working with so many talented individuals, some of whom later became my mentors, and each of whom left an indelible mark upon my life that would, perhaps, not be obvious until many years later.

At the conclusion of school, I started work as a receptionist in the banking and finance sector and quickly progressed to Personal Assistant, Executive Assistant and later, an Executive Manager. After meeting my husband just before my thirtieth birthday, I began a university degree with a major in marketing – although it quickly became apparent that pursuing a career in marketing was not quite the 'something more' I was looking for. Put simply, it failed to ignite that fire in my belly, nor triggered the butterflies that stems from pushing yourself outside of your comfort zone. Nevertheless, I continued my university studies – finally finishing with an Associate Degree in Business, which then led to a career promotion as a communications and project manager within a major international accounting firm.

At this point, life was good – I was climbing the corporate ladder and finally breaking out of the administrative roles I had effectively held since starting my formal working life. However, as the pressure and stresses of corporate life slowly replaced the years of school and dance, my 'creative' past was fast becoming a distant memory.

At thirty-two, I married the love of my life. A few years later, we were blessed with our first child and looking forward to building a 'forever home' for our growing family. Before we could break ground on our new home however, we received the news that my mother's breast cancer had returned. This had a significant impact on my family and plans for our future, as I took on the role of primary carer in addition to parenting a two-year-old, being pregnant, working full time and all whilst trying to complete my degree before the birth of my second child. Thankfully my mother did have an opportunity to hold her fourth grandchild before we lost her, and a few months later I returned from maternity leave only to be made redundant just twelve months later, following a change of leadership and subsequent restructure within the organisation.

A number of significant events had now occurred in my life over a few (too short) years. Yet, being made redundant at a moment in time when I had just lost a primary carer for my young children, together with a very flexible work environment, you could say, was the catalyst for experiencing one of 'those moments' in life where I was forced to step back and reevaluate. Being available to raise my children was a primary contributor to exploring again what that 'something more' was that I was supposed to be doing. Although I had long felt disconnected from my chosen career path, it was not until that moment of redundancy that I was finally free to explore what that 'something more' was; to be able to finally answer the question, *what do I want to be when I grow up?* And, the answer to that question came as I was organising my son's fifth birthday.

In January of 2016, planning for my son's 'Jake and the Neverland Pirates' themed birthday party was well underway. Then six months pregnant with my third child, I nevertheless spent countless hours on my computer seeking out all of the available party items required to wow our guests. One evening, I sat with my husband who had just found a 'YouTube' video of another mother who had literally purchased all of the 'Jake' themed decorations and demonstrated how best to set them up to get the most impact. My husband turned to me and said 'Wow! She's just like you!'

At that moment, a light went on and I thought to myself, *why yes, I am just like her. I could do this as a business!*

Even though I had always had a passion for creating themed events (no doubt driven by those early years of dance and some experience of event planning in my corporate life), I had never considered pursuing children's parties as a formal career. I mean, children's parties are way too much fun to be work! The feeling that this could indeed be my 'something more' however, was too strong to ignore (queue ignition of fire in belly and butterflies)! So, the next day I phoned a friend to workshop the concept. Suffice to say, she loved it, and by the end of the day I had three clients lined up to get me started on my venture. At this stage, I didn't even have a business name!

As I came up with, and discarded, name after name for my new business, I finally settled upon 'Pop the Balloon! Children's Parties & Events'. My vision for this business was to create a fun, vibrant and positive experience for the guest of honour, their family and friends – yet most of all, I wanted to leave families with a 'memory for life' that would stay with them, long after the happy squeals of delight had faded, and the cake crumbs cleared away. 'Creating memories for life' then became the marketing byline for my business and gave it its purpose and reason for being.

Starting out however, I did spend a lot of time talking to other mums who had similarly began businesses with the birth of their children as a way to earn income whilst remaining accessible to their family. I was surprised to hear that many of them started out making no money at all – and in fact, many of them only charged their clients enough to cover their expenses! As demand grew, they began to add a small mark-up - but even this remained heavily discounted and a long way from providing a sustainable income. Within approximately three years of starting their business, they all spoke of their businesses turning a corner and now that they have built solid client bases, they charge more reasonable rates that enable them to draw an income doing what they love most.

This same approach holds true with my own business. Much of my first twelve months was spent invoicing 'cost only' and mostly to clients within my family and friend network. This year however, I have followed the business decisions of many of my peers and charged a small service fee – though much of that profit is often ploughed straight back into the business.

In the almost two years since I started my business, the objectives have changed several times over. My initial vision was that I would be a 'party organiser' – someone who booked and coordinated party services on behalf of the client according to their needs. What I found however, was that clients were wanting a lot more than to hire someone purely to 'organise' their child's party. It was similarly disconcerting to learn just how expensive creating a child's party could be – especially starting out with no suppliers, no idea where the best place was to source party supplies and services from, nor did I have any clue how to avoid paying 'retail' over 'wholesale' (not to mention I had never worked in – or been exposed to – the retail trade). The more I looked at each individual 'cost per unit', coupled with adding a service fee for my time on top; the more it became obvious that the total fee proposal was putting the parties well beyond the reach of my target market.

Next, I considered how much of the party décor and styling I could create on my own. This led me down the path of party styling. Party styling is effectively taking a brief from a client to create a particular party theme (e.g. superheroes), then designing the space – from the decorations to the celebration cake, food, treat buffets and entertainment – to ensure that every element of the party comes together to create the ultimate themed experience for the client and their guests. It really is so much more than hanging balloons, placing a few paper plates and cups on a table, and coordinating glass jars filled with coloured lollies!

For the next few months, this new direction seemed to work until earlier this year, when my new client's expectations differed from my existing clients.

Now they were not only looking for party styling – they were also looking to me to stay and host party games! (Um, so you may need to picture me with my fingers in my ears for just a moment with the words 'la la la la cannot hear you' falling from my mouth...) But, if there is one thing that I have learnt early on, it is that you must constantly adapt and change to meet the market if you want to remain relevant and profitable – particularly in a service-based industry that is largely based around discretionary spend. After all, most people can put a basic party together, so I needed to consider how my design skills could be best applied to add the most value. This realisation then led me to pursue a new direction - packaging themed children's parties.

When discussing my business with potential clients, I had often found it difficult to transition the initial enquiry into actual paid business. I believe this was largely due to the clients not really understanding my business value proposition. And in truth, that was fair enough, as I wasn't always certain of it myself! But, taking the time to research my competitors service offerings did help clarify that I needed to start offering my clients 'packages' – providing clarity around what it was I was offering, so that they could see exactly what they were getting for their money. Whilst I do still manage many enquiries with clients looking for something truly spectacular – it was my accountant who enlightened me with the realisation that I cannot sustainably run a business with only 10% of clientele willing to spend large sums of money. There did need to be other layers to my business. So this year, I began creating packages for clients that were effectively a scaled down version from our larger 'signature party' offerings, with full party styling, lollies, party favour bags as well as hosted games, prizes and of course, our signature confetti filled balloon!

And fast following in the footsteps of my hosted party packages is the final layer to my business — creating an online shop that enables clients to 'shop like a party stylist' without actually hiring one. It is geared towards time poor people who are wanting to create their perfect themed event, but who lack the time and know-how to do it themselves, or who simply do not want to spend more money hiring a party stylist to create the party for them. At the time of writing, the online shop is still in the final stages of being built, but I remain confident that creating fully themed party kits will be another success story for my business.

It is fair to say however, that no one takes the decision to run their own business lightly, and many entrepreneurs start out with a genuine lack of knowledge around the trials and challenges that await. Let's face it — we most likely would not go into business at all if we knew just what those challenges would be before we started! To begin with, there is the constant juggle of family and business life. You can forget 'work-life balance', especially in the startup phase of your business. Most of my days are full of being a mum to my three children, and most nights are filled with creating marketing strategies, answering client enquiries, pricing parties, sourcing new suppliers and party décor, not to mention feeding all of the various social media platforms and website updates! All of this typically occurs once the children are in bed and the household chores complete, and usually concludes somewhere between the hours of midnight and 2am (assuming my one-year old has not woken for a 1am bottle).

With that said, I would not change my decision to run my own business for anything. Even though in many respects I am still at the start of my business journey, I am constantly amazed at what I achieve each and every day. I am there for my three children when they wake up in the morning. I am there to get their breakfast, dressed for school, daycare or for another day at home with me. I am available to go to the school book week parade, or the Mother's Day morning tea. I am able to take my children to swimming, dancing, music lessons, soccer practice and any other activity they have an interest in. I am teaching my children how to count – often by getting them to group the various party favors into piles before counting out '1' for each party bag (my future business leaders!). I am there to help with reading and school homework. I am home to make dinner for my family and I never miss the goodnight kiss (or the pleading for a second or third book before bed).

If there was one challenge however that has threatened to derail my plans for world domination – one children's party at a time – it would have to be my intense fear of failure that more or less brought my business to a standstill soon after I celebrated my first year of business. *What if the business didn't work? What if I was no good at styling children's parties? What if I had to shut it all down and go back to 'traditional' work? Who would look after my children? How would I find a job that I could love enough to want to turn up every day? What about childcare? Building our forever house? What if this?*

What if that! Out of no-where, I began to lose all interest in Pop the Balloon! and all that I worked so hard to create. I had just delivered the ultimate 'I believe in unicorns' themed party for my little girls' first birthday and was feeling a great sense of success given how well it had come together on the day. Yet post birthday party, I could no longer bring myself to invest any time at all in my business. Everything grounded to a halt in the weeks that followed. At this stage, there were no other parties on my books, nothing more to do other than to completely overhaul my website (ahem, first attempt at a business website was a little underwhelming to say the least!) and invest time, energy and money in marketing and advertising. So, without new business to focus on, all of my enthusiasm waned.

I reached the point of being so afraid of failure — that it was just better to do nothing at all and simply hope new clients would find me without my having to put myself out there or do too much to be noticed.

Mindless hours of Facebook time ensued during this period, and as if by Divine intervention, a 'mind movies' sponsored post turned up in my newsfeed. Signing up for the webinar to uncover my 'unconscious mind blockers' using 'mind movies' seemed like just the thing to discover what was holding me back from finding success in business (and it was FREE!). Suffice to say, I tuned in and spent time working through the simple activities designed to identify and break down the moments in my life that had since shaped the person I had become. As it turned out, my impressions of success (and failure) in business had stemmed from my father's failed business venture when I was in my early teens. Until that moment, I had not appreciated how the fallout of all that followed — had shaped my own views on life, nor how it had manifested itself in my mind to create a sense of 'fear' when it came to running my own business.

Having identified the issue at last, I reached out to my family to discuss more about how I was feeling. This was such a turning point for me. Discussing the issues that led to the closure of the family business brought to light a number of key business decisions that had (at the time) contributed to its demise. But more than that, my family helped me to realise that past failures are not indicative of future business success or failure. Importantly, I now appreciate that it is better to identify and recognise the issues holding you back for what they are, then take the time to work through and resolve them so that they will no longer stand in your way. In this regard, I am eternally grateful to my family and for their ongoing support, guidance and mentorship.

Running my own business has been (and continues to be) life-changing though, with the most profound impact being my own ability to problem solve better than some of the greatest minds in the world, and multi-task more efficiently than the greatest robots ever created! And whilst it can often be lonely working for yourself and by yourself – you soon learn the depth and breadth of your resilience when there are no teams of people around you to carry the day to day workload of your business – nor step in and take over on the days when you (or your children) are feeling unwell. Even those late nights caring for your new baby can be considered a terrific training ground for functioning effectively on very little sleep!

The fundamental difference here is that the effort and investment of your time and energy is directly contributing to the growth and wellbeing of your family's future. And whilst the effort of starting a small business is not without sacrifice, the longer-term gains of success for my family (coupled with the passion of doing something I truly love, rather than just doing something I am paid to do) are my most significant motivators.

With that said - even as a sole business owner, I am not without my support networks. Here I find social media has proven to be a fantastic resource for seeking out other like-minded groups and businesses to bounce ideas off and reach out to for guidance and help when I have needed it most (though wrapping your head around social media can in - and of itself – be extremely challenging to the uninitiated!) In this space, I now manage two Facebook groups. The first is 'Party Stylists Australia', which I created in anticipation of attracting other party businesses like mine whose primary objective is to plan, create, style and theme parties and events for their clients. I established this group with the sole purpose of providing party stylists and/or event planners across Australia with a place where they can collaborate, share ideas and inspiration, seek out suppliers for their business and otherwise encourage our industry and each other to flourish in our local Australian market. "The second is 'The Party Shed Buy Swap and Sell' which is a bit like an online marketplace for people to on-sell their unwanted party supplies as well as connect with other likeminded 'over the top' party people and party professionals.

Aside from the obvious opportunities and benefits of connecting with tribes of like-minded individuals on social media, my children's party business would not have progressed at the pace it has without the incredible support from my husband and invaluable mentorship from my brother-in-law and other professionals I have worked with during my career. Although often frustrated with my party props and supplies steadily taking over his garage, my husband has remained unfailing in his support of my business venture, even to the point of taking on the role of primary investor. Every business (no matter how small), needs an injection of working capital to get it started and, together with my brother-in-law (himself a highly successful marketing professional), I have been twice blessed to have both the financial backing and appropriate business advice and guidance needed to help navigate the early stages of running my business.

Yet even with this amazing collective of business professionals, family, mothers and fellow entrepreneurs, my children's party business would never have made it off the ground without the support and encouragement (and the odd 'shove' in the right direction) of one very special friend. It was this friend whom ensured I had three clients waiting to engage my services as a children's party planner within the first twenty-four hours of conceiving my business; who stayed up late into the evenings with me reviewing my business purpose, objectives, vision and content for my website — pointing out what was fabulous and what needed more work. Who constantly encouraged me to keep going when I felt overwhelmed or that perhaps this wouldn't work as a business after all. And who, perhaps most importantly, was (and continues to be) my right-hand — standing side by side with me through each and every party set up, change in business direction and any other mad idea my creative brain can conceive. My sincerest thanks to you, Rebecca!

I genuinely believe that every entrepreneur needs a 'Rebecca' in their life — whether that person is their mother, sister, husband, friend or fellow colleague — you really can scale the highest mountains when you surround yourself with positive influencers and advocators of your business, who want nothing more for you than to see you succeed.

Despite what I have achieved for myself personally and professionally, my energy and passion to be constantly challenged has already driven me toward scaling my next mountain which entails taking the blueprints from my existing business and expanding into the broader party market. The name 'Party Utopia' came to me one morning as I was engaged in the usual chore of hanging the washing on the line (of all places for inspiration to strike). I had already received several requests from clients wanting me to create their perfect engagement or bridal shower space based on my portfolio of work – however I had declined the offers on the basis that it was outside the remit of my children's business (and to be frank, outside of my comfort zone too). However, with the inspiration of a business name; the size and scope of the broader party styling and event market seemed to be a natural fit for the next stage of my business. So, in October 2017, Party Utopia Events officially launched with a gorgeous 'Mad Hatters Tea Party' inspired bridal shower. Whilst the initial business objective will centre around creating incredible parties and events for my clients and their guests who are looking for an amazing experience celebrating those moments in life that mean the most to them – I cannot wait to see if this business will continually evolve down new pathways, as was the case with my children's party business.

In reflecting on my life thus far, I now understand how every facet of it has led me to fulfil my 'something more'. The creativity to come up with, and deliver, exciting party themes and concepts was clearly derived from those early years of dancing, choreographing, creating costumes and being inspired by other significant entertainment empires — most notably for me the incredible world of 'Disney' as no other organisation on earth creates entertainment 'magic' the way that they do. The business acumen to run and manage my businesses shines through from my 20+ years as an executive assistant, working with and supporting some of the best strategic leaders and corporate professionals within the Australian finance industry — so too the academic skills and qualifications that came from my business studies at university. It can even be said that losing my beloved mother has strengthened my resilience; having the ability to bounce back from the worst that life can throw at you is definitely a key skill to develop if you are wanting to be successful in business. Yet, I believe that it was being made redundant from my role as a communications and project manager that truly contributed to my starting a business, as without that 'shove' from a company I was very proud to be an employee of, I might never have had the courage to discover my true passion and calling.

So, with this in mind, I encourage you — the mum and future entrepreneur — to take a moment to reflect on all that you have accomplished in your life.

Can you see the patterns? Is there anything holding you back? Can you see how each decision you have made and life experience forms part of a greater purpose for your life? Even if you have yet to discover your 'something more', give yourself the space and freedom to explore what is possible — and do not ignore those life experiences that have embedded themselves in your mind; causing mischief and mayhem and otherwise potentially holding you back from your dream career! Instead, pull out the magnifying glass and take a closer look, and be brave in dealing with whatever the magnifying glass reveals.

A few years ago, I read a quote on Facebook from the highly successful entrepreneur – Richard Branson. His words of wisdom were essentially to accept every opportunity that comes your way. Even if you are not sure that you can do it, say 'yes', then figure out how to do it afterward. As a result, I now live every day with Richard's words in mind – even on the days when I really don't believe I can rise to the challenge of whatever my businesses are throwing at me! But more than that, be grateful for the failures and the set-backs that come with being an entrepreneur … after all, these are the bricks in the road that forge the path to your future success.

Rochelle

We need to accept that we won't always make the right decisions, that we'll screw up royally sometimes - understanding that failure is not the opposite of success, it's part of success."

— Arianna Huffington, Editor of Huffington Post

Samantha Young

Human Psychology

My name is Samantha Young. Everyone calls me Sam, except for my two gorgeous daughters, who call me Mum. I own Human Psychology, one of Adelaide's largest psychological services and training solutions providers. Our mission is to help people to think, feel and perform better to realise their potential. We work with organisations, teams and individuals using scientifically-validated methodologies to enhance employee wellbeing and engagement. Services include design and delivery of training workshops, Employee Assistance Program counselling, critical incident management, clinical counselling, executive coaching and complex HR consulting. We have recently taken our programs national, running 'Aspiring Women' in Melbourne. We have twelve staff. In 2018, we are launching an e-learning business and will continue to take our training solutions national.

The company started in 2007 with two other business partners in a small rented office on a part-time basis. I have been the sole owner for nearly eighteen months after my business partner decided to resign from the business in May 2016. We have never borrowed money to fund expansion or used our over-draft. Over the past ten years, while the business has grown, I have learned a huge number of lessons about building a business whilst parenting as a single mum.

Know your numbers and have a plan. A lot of women I work with hate numbers. They label themselves 'bad at maths' and don't understand financials. For your business to survive and thrive, it is critical that you have a basic grasp on business accounting. This includes understanding cash flow, profit and loss statements, accounts receivable and budgets. I have seen too many business that have clients and work go under because they didn't invoice, collect debts, invest in marketing to win new business and charge enough for what they were doing. You can work extremely hard and still lose money. Avoiding the cash flow crisis starts with having a solid business plan that includes financial projections that are reviewed regularly.

I have always been wary of taking on debt as my risk-profile is conservative. If you are going to borrow for your business, get professional advice and set up a company structure that protects your family assets. Borrowing against your house is a risky decision, as is using credit cards to fund growth. A good rule of thumb is to have three months operating costs available in the bank out of cash flow.

I am also a strong believer in insurance. I was diagnosed with breast cancer nearly five years ago and without business and income protection insurance, my family and company would have been in financial dire straits. I pay for quality legal and accounting advice and have a business coach to 'reality check' my decisions. Paying for expertise can seem costly up front but can save massive headaches down the track. No one ever wins going to court, except the lawyers.

Having a bold vision of where you want to take your company provides direction and motivation.

Bigger is not always better, but too many female business owners limit themselves from scaling their business for the wrong reasons. This is why women will only apply for a job if they meet 100% of the job criteria and yet most men will apply if they meet just 50%! Make sure you are charging what you are worth. I used to be fearful of raising my hourly Executive Coaching rate and worried people would think it was too much, but when I charged more it created a perception that I was *worth* more. Be aware of your margins and try not to compete on price. If I have a client who is super-price sensitive, I tend to conclude that we are the wrong supplier for them and/or I haven't demonstrated the value sufficiently of the premium service we are providing.

Be patient and work hard. Build on solid foundations with durable ideas rather than looking for a trendy and quick way of making money. Reputations take years to build and minutes to lose. It will take time and serious repeated hard work for your ideas to start turning into cash flow. Learn how to hustle. A verb and a noun, 'hustle' implies that you're constantly moving or pushing towards a goal and getting your ideas out in to the world. This might mean putting yourself on the line again and again, being open to rejection and failure and executing not over-planning. I honestly think there is no substitute for plain old hard work.

Get comfortable with marketing and self-promotion. Most of us would rather stick a pen in our eye than talk about our achievements and promote ourselves, but working for yourself, you *are* your business. Personal branding is critical in the digital age and this includes our social media presence, integrated marketing efforts and building networks. I have found that women have a tendency to expect that if they work really hard and do a great job, then that is enough for success to flow. It is not. Investing time and effort in communicating your 'why' to your target market is just as important as actually doing the work. It is a difficult juggle finding the time to complete work whilst also getting out there to win new business, but you need to have work in the pipeline. Winning new clients is usually harder than really looking after your existing ones. Think about what problems you can solve for them and add value wherever possible. I believe that people do business with people they like and trust, and this comes down to quality relationships.

Work-life integration. Don't strive for work-life balance, it doesn't exist! It implies a perfect static state that is rarely achieved for more than a day juggling all of life's competing demands. Work-life integration is about making conscious choices and trade-offs and trying to blend the two worlds of work and personal life together in a way that works for you. Sometimes, work needs to take precedence; sometimes family demands do. Embrace the chaos backed up by military-grade planning and organisational skills, and work out what you can delegate, drop or do differently based on your personal values about how you want to invest your precious time.

Instead of seeking strict separation between work and personal life, we can allow the lines to blur more through use of technology and flexible work practices, and shift work around on dimensions of time and space. The boundaries between work and home-life are increasingly indistinct and we need to rethink the traditional concept of work and life as two separate entities. True balance is rarely found whilst harmony through work-life integration is attainable. Sometimes personal time will interrupt work and vice versa. Balance infers even distribution of time but the splitting of time, effort and energy between work and home is always uneven and unpredictable.

Instead of thinking about what work you can integrate into your home life, try to focus on the larger picture and integrate all areas of your life the best way that you can. The ultimate aim is to optimise how you use your time, so you can fulfill your needs, both in your work and your personal life. Try to be real, whole and innovative:

Real - be authentic by clarifying what is important to you

Whole - act with integrity by recognising how the different parts if your life (work, home, community, self) affect each other

Innovative - be creative and experiment with how things get done in ways that are good for you and for the people around you. Then plan your time ruthlessly in a way that reflects your priorities.

> **"There is no such thing as work-life balance. Everything worth fighting for unbalances your life."**
> Alain de Botton

Guilt. This leads me on to the most crippling of emotions for working mothers. Guilt. All of the 'shoulds' that we burden ourselves with trying to be everything to everyone.

We compare ourselves to social media perfection and feel like we are not good enough. But you are, you are enough, and you only need to succeed at your personal definition of success, based on your own core values. Putting yourself first sometimes is not selfish, it is necessary to sustain your energy levels and wellbeing. Your needs are important too, and it will not hurt your family to not get instant gratification all of the time.

Understanding that some mothers work and work for themselves is an important life lesson for our children.

Society loves to punish mothers. Everything seems to be our fault. If you choose to work as a mother, then you are 'selfish' and not doing the right thing by your family. This makes working mums try even harder to achieve everything perfectly and it is making us stressed, sad and exhausted. My grand-mother had a saying: "Dear, don't nail yourself to the cross, it is really hard to get the last nail in". Sacrificing oneself on the altar of a perfect mother image modelled on last century is bad for our families, relationships and children, not to mention our personal wellbeing. It risks raising entitled children who lack resilience. Having a career or working (aka earning money to live for most) is not mutually exclusive to being a 'good mother', whatever that label currently means. Where are the angst-ridden articles from fathers bemoaning their work-life balance struggle, parental guilt and 'bad father' labels? Apparently 'bad mothers' put chocolate cake in their children's lunch boxes whereas to earn the 'bad father' label, you basically need to murder your entire family. Even then, that is justified too often on the basis of provocation. I'm just done with this bullshit. You know what is right for you and your family. Just do that.

Imposter syndrome. Imposter Syndrome is a collection of feelings of inadequacy that remain even in the face of information that indicates that the opposite is true. It is experienced as chronic self-doubt that can be summarised as "I am a fraud, and everyone is about to find out." The term Impostor Syndrome was coined to describe this way of feeling back in the 1980's. Researchers believe that up to 70% of people have suffered from it at some point. Impostor Syndrome is typically associated with highly achieving, highly successful people. Women experiencing Impostor Syndrome may be less willing to put themselves forward, feeling that they are not qualified, by:

- not applying for jobs, promotions, pay rises and other employment opportunities
- disclaiming or understating their experience/skill
- experiencing nervousness about talking to others in their field
- feeling like a fraud
- worrying that someone will find out their lack of qualifications and fire them
- having higher stress
- over-preparing for tasks
- downplaying successes to chance or luck
- filtering out positive comments and compliments
- not sharing their achievements and successes and failing to self-promote

Accept that you had a role in your success and learn to internalise your achievements and successes by acknowledging that it was not all down to good luck, timing, other people or external circumstances. Try to be less concerned about yourself and what others are thinking about you. By genuinely trying to help someone else and focusing on creating and sharing value in your interactions with others, you will shift your focus away from yourself.

Giving your best is not the same thing as *being* your best 100% of the time. There is a big difference between trying to improve yourself and having to be better than everyone else. Overcoming Imposter Syndrome requires self-acceptance. It is not about lowering your standards, it is about resetting them to a realistic level that does not leave you forever striving and feeling inadequate.

Take responsibility for your successes as equally you do your failures. Try writing a list of all the major things you've accomplished over the last few years. Look at the list – you deserved your successes, didn't you? Also, write down the positive things people have said about you and your work, and review this list regularly.

Learn to respect your own experience and stop comparing yourself so harshly with others. Author Iyanla Vanzant believes that "comparison is an act of violence against the self." Comparisons tend to be subjective, biased and rarely helpful. Realise that no one actually really knows what they are doing! You are not an imposter for trying something that might not work.

Being wrong and making mistakes does not make you an imposter. They make you human.

Sometimes, faking it does not make you a fraud. For example, if you smile your body will produce 'happy' chemicals and actually make you feel happier. If you behave assertively and confidently even though you may feel nervous, others will react to you differently and reinforce your self-confidence. Neuroplasticity means that you can shape your brain by faking behaviour until you feel differently. This does not mean being inauthentic or wearing multiple masks. Who you are is enough already.

Build and access support networks. Running your own business can be lonely and exhausting. It is tempting to think that you have to do everything if it is going to be done properly. And it can feel like a sign of weakness to ask for help. It is actually a sign of strength. You cannot maintain your wellbeing long-term without drawing on an extensive network of support.

I am fortunate enough to be able to outsource a lot of things and I delegate as hard as I can. There are still days when I look at the weeds in the garden, dirty windows, pile of ironing and notices for school events that I can't make and feel overwhelmed. And then, the dog gets sick or car breaks down and the whole carefully organised disaster that feels like my life sometimes seems to come crashing down. So, I have learned to let go of the unimportant things and not sweat the small stuff. Most things are small stuff. The health and wellbeing of our loved ones and ourselves is the big stuff. Everything else can wait.

If you are trying to choose between running a bubble bath and having a glass of wine, and reading a book, or doing the ironing, please choose the first option.

Have fun. I know, right, this one sounds silly, but don't under-estimate it! Having a sense of humour and perspective are life savers when the going gets tough. Things will get tough. Clients won't pay, staff will leave, the electricity or GST bill comes in, the kids get sick, you get sick. Play and fun are not just for kids, they are necessary activities for our wellbeing and for creativity to flourish.

Your why. Why are you doing this? What is your life purpose? Knowing the answer to this question will keep you going through the tough days/weeks/months of being self-employed. I am a strong believer in the diagram below. You don't find your purpose. You make it. Through self-reflection, consistent action and facing fear. Start with unpacking your core values and identify strengths, and then use these as the foundation for goal setting. Defining success on our own terms is scary and hard, but crucial to running your own business.

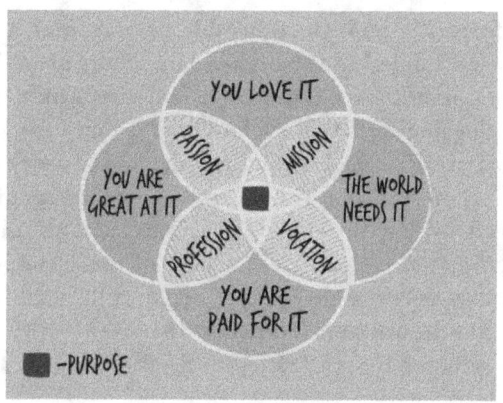

Do what scares you. Fear is one of our most important instincts. All of us are alive today because our ancestors were really good at predicting and reacting to threat. The ability to detect threat in our environments has served us well over the millennia, enabling us to pass on our genes. This is our prime directive, to make copies of our DNA and survive long enough for our children to do the same. Human babies require a huge amount of protection and education to survive long enough to replicate, and fear helps us do this successfully. The problem with fear in the modern world is it gets it wrong. Our brains now detect threat where it does not exist in reality, and this makes us feel threatened when we don't need to be. Anxious, stressed, worried and hyper-vigilant. I think fear motivates a sizeable proportion of our choices and behaviour. It is often our 'lizard' brains dictating this choice, not our rational pre-frontal cortex.

I love the question, "What would you do if you were not afraid?" Be really honest with yourself when reflecting on this question. Would you quit your job and pursue your passion? Would you tell your partner how you truly feel about them and allow yourself to be vulnerable? Would you care less about what you thought other people were thinking about you and voice your beliefs and opinions, even if they might not be popular? Fear can stop us pursing what is meaningful and important to us, as much as it pretends to be keeping us safe from harm. It becomes a miscued emotion triggering at the prospect of threat to our self-esteem like a poorly calibrated car alarm. Our brains react to perceived psychological threat in the same way as to physical threat. Our fight-flight system gets jammed on, our bodies flood with stress chemicals and we then try to avoid the threat. We understandably avoid what scares us.

But, what if the threat is actually something we really want, but it is scary?

It is perhaps scary because we aren't certain about the outcome, we can't guarantee success and we may therefore fail or make a mistake. It seems safer to stay with the 'devil we know', the certainty of what we can predict and understand. Staying within known parameters, we think that we can minimise anxiety and fear. On the face of it, that seems like a sensible idea. The problem is, we don't know what is going to happen tomorrow and we don't know what other people are thinking. We are trying to control two things we *can't* know – the future and other people's thoughts.

In the last few years, I have consciously chosen to do things that have scared me witless. I climbed the Sydney Harbour Bridge, I abseiled down a building for charity, I went cage diving with sharks, I went on ABC radio, I crawled in tunnels in Vietnam, I gave my child an adrenalin pen when she had an anaphylactic reaction, I started running a business on my own, I re-evaluated friendships and relationships and I walked away from business contracts. Many of these things may not be scary for you, but they were for me. These things were easy compared to choices I see my clients make every day. Like taking on graded exposure treatment plans for anxiety that entail facing terror daily in the hope that their brains will learn that what they are most fear is really not that bad.

I have a beautiful friend who had been secretly painting. She is genuinely talented, and her art is fabulous. Last year, she held her first joint exhibition and was terrified. So terrified that she kept dropping the prices of her pieces. At the opening of the exhibition, I was shocked to see how cheaply she had priced her hard work and talent. I questioned her about his and begged her to increase the prices to reflect her worth. I learned that she again dropped prices on some of her large pieces as they had not sold. A mutual friend offered to display her art in his winery and my friend balked at this offer, especially at his directive that she needed to triple her pricing and price the large piece markedly higher to 'anchor' the collection at the right value point. "But it makes me so nervous,

Sam!" she exclaimed, "what if no one likes it?". Ah, but what if they do, my friend?

Don't Wait. Don't wait. Tell those you love today, right now, what they mean to you. Make time for listening, sharing, laughter and fun. People are what matter and meaningful relationships are fundamentally what gives our lives purpose at the end of the day. And, pursue your dreams. Don't have regrets about what you didn't do or say. Please stop waiting for the right time and embrace your possible future today.

> **"Waiting for the fish to bite or waiting for wind to fly a kite. Or waiting around for Friday night or waiting perhaps for their Uncle Jake or a pot to boil or a better break or a string of pearls or a pair of pants or a wig with curls or another chance. Everyone is just waiting."**
> Dr Seuss

My youngest daughter recently asked me out of the blue, "Mummy, if you weren't doing your work, what job would you most love to have?". I had to think about my answer for a while and ended up responding, "I would still do what I do now". What a gift she gave me in that moment! I realised I was lucky enough to be spending my time doing something I loved. I hope you find the same.

Samantha

Susanna Heiskanen

Tuutu

My journey to becoming an entrepreneur started during my childhood in Finland. I had lots of family members who owned or worked in small businesses. It seemed to be the thing to do in rural 1980's Finland where starting up a company was easy, and it felt that everyone was doing it. However, when recession hit in the late 1980's many businesses failed and had to close. Even worse, people like my parents who had guaranteed loans ended up paying not just their own mortgage, but also someone else's business loan. This should have kept me from going on the journey of starting up my own business but rather than deter me, I found it all very interesting. Starting to work as a teen in my cousin's nursery, picking strawberries and working as a cashier was my first touch of the working world. I remember the day I bought my first bike with the money I had earned. The feeling of achievement from getting the money to pay for something so precious was priceless. I still have the bike at my parents' house in Finland, reminding me that hard work brings rewards.

Once I left Finland to work in London in 1999, the thought of having my own business was buried under the excitement of living the life in London in my early twenties. After few more years, I had a comfy corporate job, a lovely boyfriend and we had just bought our own home together. What more would you want to have? I started to feel that I was ready to move on after eight years in London. Opportunity came, and I was transferred to Sydney with my company and after some negotiations, I knew this was the right move for me. I had been studying in London whilst working and I completed my degree in International Relations with the thought that I would be moving into working in a NGO. Once I had arrived in the land down under, I remember my first evening here walking around Circular Quay and taking in the view, thinking that I must be the luckiest girl to be able to call this home.

Even at that point, I had not been thinking about owning my own business, but when I started working in Sydney I every now and then dreamt how lovely it would be to be your own boss and work for yourself. I was thinking about areas of business that I was good at and as at this point in time I was a Quality Manager, I was entertaining the idea of consulting in this field. However, after making some enquiries I soon realised that I had to have much more experience to be able to start up my own consultancy business. I discarded the thought of having a consultancy business but the process of starting my own company had already taken a hold at the back of my mind.

One of the reasons I moved to Australia was to complete my private pilot license. My passion for flying comes from my childhood where I had pictures of planes on my bedroom wall, whilst my friends had rock stars and actors. I was always envious of those kids who got to go on long distance holidays in planes. I was determined that I was going to be flying my own plane one day. Once in Australia, I saved money to allow me to complete my Private Pilot License and then moved onwards to complete my Commercial Pilot License. Once I started flying I soon realised that becoming a pilot was a dream come true. I felt relaxed and at ease when flying a plane. It's not everyone's cup of tea, but I was having a blast. At the same time, I was promoted in my corporate job and I was away long periods of time and I found it difficult to keep my flying hours going whilst away for weeks, if not months at the time. I persevered however and continued clocking up the hours and passing exams slowly but surely.

It was in 2011 that I started to think about my future. I was contemplating finishing off my private pilot's license by resigning from my job and just concentrating on flying instead. However, fate stepped in and I realised that I was pregnant with my first son. This unexpected joy forced me to study even harder and continue flying - almost until the very end of my pregnancy - to make sure that I got all necessary hours and experience under my belt until my flying would have to be put on hold for a while. My flight instructor was mindful when we planned our navigational exercises to have an extra airport in between the points just in case. I welcomed my son in September 2012 and I was back flying three months later. My son was an easy child and whilst I was nursing him, I started to think about what I wanted to do next with my life, as getting a pilot license obviously was not fueling that hunger anymore.

The idea of returning to my corporate life was not appetizing at all.

I could not face being away for weeks at the time anymore, and things that I used to enjoy like travel, seeing new places and cultures were no longer the thing for me. I started to crave something else. I felt that as much as I loved my son, I wanted to do something else as well. I have always worked and being a mother, I just did not find it challenging. Or, let's just say that I was not stimulated enough by the conversations and actions I was taking. After over a year on maternity leave, I discovered that I was pregnant again. I had my final flying exam the same week and once I landed, my instructor congratulated me, telling me that I had passed. I in return, told him that I was pregnant again. He was happy, but I think he was happier that I passed so that he did not have to think about flying with me whilst I was pregnant again.

This time around my pregnancy was not easy and I was having morning, day and evening sickness, so I quickly had to abandon the idea of flying whilst pregnant like I had with my first one. We welcomed our second son in November 2014. This time around, motherhood was not as easy. Looking after a toddler and a new born was harder than I thought. Thankfully, I have a very hands-on husband who took on more responsibility by looking after the older one.

Whilst at home with my second child, I started to think some more about what I wanted to do. Starting a business sounded intriguing, but I could not decide what shape or form it would take. My sister had suggested to me when I had my first son that I should start producing the Finnish baby box in Australia. I was not even remotely interested at the time, being a sleep deprived new mother. However now, I was thinking what a cool idea it was and yes of course, I wanted to produce the Finnish baby box here in Australia.

The Finnish Baby Box has its roots in 1930's Finland. The box started as a basket full of baby clothing that was passed from family to family as babies were born. The clothes were in a wooden basket that was used as a place for the baby to sleep as well. The baby box concept evolved over time and soon it became apparent to the health authorities of the benefits of giving the basket and providing health education to mothers at the same time. This charity basket was taken over by the Health Ministry and it was made into more of a formal process with women having to attend pre-natal clinics in order to be eligible for the baby box. The pre-natal clinics (called the Neuvola system) are still going strong to this day. By 1949, the Finnish government passed a law that every woman throughout the country - irrespective of their socio-economic status - would get one of these boxes. This 'every child matters' policy is still going strong and over the years, the Finnish Government has given out over four million baby boxes to parents to be. I still recall some of the items that were part of the year when I was born and the colour of the green box as we used to play with the box and the contents when I was older.

This baby box concept promotes equality and also provides a safe place for the baby to sleep. It ticked all the boxes for me as to what I wanted to do next with my career. I wanted to start up a company to produce this in Australia. Needless to say, I was excited. I started my research and began to talk to my Finnish friend Laura on how this product could become a reality in Australia. After some research, it was very clear that there were only a few suppliers who would be willing to make the actual cardboard box. The complexity of the design and machinery required meant we had to make decisions on cut, design, and colour early on in the design phase. We spent hour after hour talking, planning, setting up our website, writing emails, chasing providers and everything that goes with setting up a business. I found that the fun part was meeting people in person and we were lucky enough to come across some incredible supporting brands early on in our journey. These local Australian brands have been rallying for us and supporting us through social media ever since. Something that I have learnt is that no brand exists without the help of others.

After nine months of careful planning and putting our lives on hold, we gave birth to Tuutu in August 2016.

Our vision had become reality and we clocked our first sales in the first week of business. We were thrilled! This could only mean that we had hit gold. However, silence was the next thing. We had no sales for weeks after. We were desperately trying to figure what was wrong. Why was no one buying our boxes? Have we got it wrong? We were analysing everything from our website to marketing tactics etc. In the end, it was a realisation that starting and running a business is a marathon not a 100m sprint. I have since learnt from many business owners that you need perseverance and persistence, amongst other things. Success does not come overnight but requires years of hard work. We had thought that this box would be the next big thing among Australian parents, but the reality was that it was a niche product and we needed to re-think some of our marketing tactics.

While this thought process was going on, we were also stuck with the fact that we started our website with iPhone photos as the photographer that we had employed was unable to supply decent photos. We had to get these images redone. My advice through this experience is that you need to get professional photos by a product photographer. Do not try to cut corners with your website, as the look and feel of it is what people will see when deciding whether or not to buy your product.

Over the next few months, we started to see an increase in website traffic and again another learning, that the SEO of your website does not appear on the first page of a Google search as soon as you publish the page. To help this we started to look at other areas of the business and how we could increase the traffic and sales without putting too much money into it. But again, another learning: to make money, you need to spend money. You cannot expect to get a high return for your investment if you spend pennies; the reality is that you will get pennies back. We are still exploring marketing tactics and fine tuning the adverts, however the majority of our traffic and sales is driven by online advertising.

After going for nearly a year, it was becoming apparent that the partnership with my friend Laura was not working. She had moved to the US with her family during the launch and as much as we were trying to get the business working together, it became clear to me that she needed to be in Australia in order to make the business work. Laura took a step back to concentrate on her family and life in the US and this enabled us to make some changes to Tuutu and move forward with a new determination.

Having kids at an older age and finding myself running my own business was nothing short of a miracle, looking back at where I have come from. My parents were not wealthy, and although we were never short of anything when growing up, there was always this careful planning that had to take place for everything to be covered month to month. Perhaps this environment of careful planning and making sure we had money has driven my need to succeed and impress my peers, friends and family. I was recently interviewed for a study about women in business in Australia and the researcher called me a firecracker. I took that as a compliment. I am certainly not lost for words; I feel the need to succeed because so many before me have not. When you start looking at women in business, there are many who have the inclination, but not so many who actually go and do it. I find that there is a comradeship amongst female business owners here in Australia. People are supportive of each other, form collaborations and speak out for one another. If I would have started my business journey from within Finland I think it would have been a really different environment and outcome. I certainly would not have started a baby box company and I would not be where I am today.

The future for Tuutu is bright. I can see us developing other product lines and developing the Tuutu brand itself further. I am also enjoying the flexibility of working from home and being a mother. My son is starting school in January, which will be a change of pace for all of us. Adapting to a new routine will be a challenge, but owning your own business makes life so much easier, and to be able to work the hours around your kids needs is a blessing. I would not have my life any other way. If I could offer one piece of advice to any mother reading this and wondering if she can go and start a business of her own, it would be, "Go and do it!". If you fail and doubt yourself, pick yourself up and do it anyway. You are the master of your own destiny.

I just love bossy women. I could be around them all day. To me, bossy is not a pejorative term at all. It means somebody's passionate and engaged and ambitious and doesn't mind learning.

-Amy Poehler

Talita Sheedy

Lahlita Natural Medicine

My name is Talita and I am from Coolum Beach on the Sunshine Coast, Queensland. Here I live with my husband, Paul and son, Jet. We are a beach loving family and are lucky enough to live walking distance to the beach, so we can see and smell the ocean daily. Coincidently, both my husband and I grew up three hours inland in Toowoomba, however our combined love for the beach saw us move coastal while we were still young. I originally moved to the Gold Coast where I studied to be a Naturopath before moving to the Sunshine Coast once I completed my studies, and soon after got married in 2014.

Moving to the Sunshine Coast was a fabulous step forward for my career. I was able to create a role for myself at a residential mental health program, where I stayed on developing the medical department which now has three naturopaths, three nutritionists as part of the team and also works with integrated doctors. This role, with a lot of hard work and hours, landed me the position of Head of Medical after three years.

During this time, I also grew my own business, Lahlita Natural Medicine, where I opened my clinic in Coolum Beach. It was a very busy time, however before children I had the opportunity to do so. To help stay grounded, yoga was my vice and connection to personal development. I decided to take it further and studied to be a yoga teacher in 2015.

Yoga helped to open my mind to a different philosophy and way of life that would later assist with my parenting; not to mention the benefits of including yoga into my daily life improved my coping mechanisms with stress, fitness and strength. The yoga and natural medicine combination was perfect for me specialising in mental health. Mental health has always been a part of my life with family members dealing with it and also suffering from depression and anxiety myself in my early twenties. Through experiencing the conventional medical system with limited outcomes, to finding natural medicine and seeing the changes in my life, it became a driver for me to study natural medicine and specialise in mental health myself. There were limited naturopaths that specialised in this area initially; however thankfully now that mental health is spoken about more commonly, there are increased options of treatment available. I was finding the majority of my patients in private clinic were seeking help for mental health, women's hormonal issues and child to teenage health. This happened organically and led to my next specialty in pregnancy and women's hormones, though it didn't take off in a huge way until I fell pregnant myself.

Once I fell pregnant at the end of 2015, my life and focus certainly changed. Not in the way of my passion towards mental health – if anything, this grew stronger in hope to create a healthier society for my child – but my focus did divert to pregnancy, hormones, and the emotional changes that go along with it. It identified the importance of prevention of mental health issues from preconception, by supporting neurotransmitter growth and functioning while still in the womb. This also led on to prevent a future of mental health conditions for the baby and supporting the pregnancy to set the mum up for that challenging post-natal period.

To carry forward my new focus and passion, I enrolled in a Pre/Post Natal Yoga teacher training course in Byron Bay.

At nineteen weeks and then again at twenty-five weeks pregnant, I was learning how to teach pregnancy yoga and mums/bubs yoga classes. This may not have been optimal while still working at the mental health program, plus running my own business, however when I have a strong interest in an area, it is difficult for me not to step into that space and learn what I can. It turned out it was very helpful for my own pregnancy and I learnt a lot about self-care, yoga to support pregnancy and birth, and empowerment of women, all of which was all very helpful and relevant for my own pregnancy journey. Also, I am very thankful for the wonderful women that shared that space with me. My pregnancy brought up a lot of old emotions and anxiety that I thought I had processed, and those beautiful women helped to support me in my pregnancy and birthing choices. Being a naturopath and living quite a 'natural' lifestyle, my views were rather different to most mums at home, as they were quite conventional. For example, I was planning on a home birth and being in the Byron area, I was supported greatly with this decision.

So, as you can see, the yoga teacher training was not simply for career gain, it also immensely helped my personal growth that I felt was very important when looking into my career. I feel incredibly lucky to have chosen a career path that I am super passionate about and love learning more and more. This way it doesn't feel like work; more so just living my loves each day. It's so rewarding having the knowledge of natural medicine, nutrition, yoga and mindfulness and how beneficial that is for my own family and now, being a mum. If I were to stop being a naturopath and yoga teacher today, the financial investment over the years towards my career wouldn't have gone to waste due to how it now supports the wellness of my family.

During my pregnancy, I decided to blog each week about my own personal experience and also what happens each week for the baby, and what kind of issues may arise and how to treat them naturally. I gave nutrition and yoga tips throughout my weekly blogs, plus the sharing of my personal experience was a great way for me to stay connected to my pregnancy, and also for my son to potentially read in the future for what I went through while carrying him. This writing/blogging helped open more windows of opportunity with other blogs as well as businesses asking me to write articles and guest blogs for them. I thoroughly love writing, as I've always been someone who has journaled, however now my writing can help others, which gives it more meaning.

After Jet was born, I continued working as Head of Medical at the mental health program, as well as seeing my own clients and teaching the odd fill in yoga class. However, I found a need to do more. Well, not consciously, it just happened. Whilst I was researching introducing foods to my son at six months of age, I quickly began to notice how outdated the information was and how it conflicted with the latest knowledge we had on nutrition and babies. Also, with the high levels of behavioural disorders in children, I felt the need to focus at the beginning, when we start foods. Through specialising in mental health for all those years, I acknowledged the importance of digestive health due to the gut-brain connection and questioned why we weren't focusing on this from day one of introducing foods to our children, especially with the concerning rates of behaviour disorders, lowered immunity and also the long-term prevention of mental health. I tapered it right back to ensure the gut heals correctly from day one. Hence, my book was born. So yes, while working at the mental health program and in my own business, I decided to write a book with up to date, evidence-based research of introducing foods to babies with the focus of boosting natural immunity and prevention of behavioural disorders. This was a lot of work; however, I was in this chapter at the same time as giving Jet foods, and with the added passion, this work did not seem draining at all.

I was excited to be writing something that would help other mums, babies and hopefully the future health of the general population.

Through writing this book, it was clear that my passion and interest for my career had certainly shifted from focusing solely on mental health and instead, to prevention from the earliest ages. I loved when a couple would come to me for preconception health, which truly does give the best opportunity for the health of the baby. I would then support these families through pregnancy, post-natal, then beyond with the milestones of the babies to children. With this shift, plus Jet becoming more of a little boy, I decided it was time to step away from the mental health program as Head of Medical, and instead focus on my upcoming new passions of writing, educating and empowering mums about pregnancy, foods and supporting the health of their children. I also loved the extra time I was able to spend with Jet, and actually be present with him. It saddened me to think the time I had with Jet while I was working like crazy was a blur, however I was thankful at the same time that I was able to realise this necessity of change and begin to embrace these wonderful early years with him. I followed my heart, which was actually a difficult step to take in today's society when we consider finances as a priority.

The financial side was always a challenge for decision making with my career - follow the money or follow the passion? Whilst I had been lucky to combine the two over the years, there was always that concern when only working for yourself and not having that weekly pay check coming in. However now, I am a firm believer that if you follow your heart and passion, you will always have enough financial support to do what you require. It doesn't come easy though - you still have to put in the work and keep pushing and striving to succeed.

I always dreamt of having my own business. It is so fulfilling, and as much as it is a lot of extra work also, I feel it is worth the reward. Looking back to when I first opened my own business, it seemed quite crazy to be working full time hours at the mental health program, however having the door open to my own business kept opportunities open for me, rather than having all my eggs in one basket. It started off slowly as I was not only new to the coast, but also a new naturopath, and had not advertised my business, mostly due to lack of time. I would see a few clients a week of my own until my reputation grew, and as word of mouth spread my client list grew and grew.

For advertising my business, I didn't do too much to be honest, other than having a Facebook page, a flyer at the post office and a local healthy café, and I also did a letterbox drop once of over five-hundred flyers and had not one client from it. For me, all my business has come from word of mouth and these are the best referrals to get. I do now have a website from when I started blogging, however people still need to hear about me to be directed to check it out. From building reputation and connections with other practitioners, I receive referral clients from a local doctor, a chiropractor, two acupuncturists, midwives, physiotherapists, yoga teachers, massage therapists and other naturopaths that feel their clients would benefit seeing me, due to my specialties.

From here, I hope to continue on my own business path with new opportunities arising. I would love to continue writing and perhaps publish another book about natural health through pregnancy, then speak at seminars or conferences to inspire other practitioners and mums about what I have found over my journey. I will definitely continue to teach yoga - especially prenatal and mums yoga, as this is where my heart currently lays. Yoga keeps me grounded and mindful, which I certainly need seeing as I'm a pretty big dreamer. I need the reality to keep me focused on one day at a time. I hope my work takes me in the direction to create a change for our children and how we look at behaviour disorders and immune compromised conditions, in hope to have a brighter stronger future for our children and also, their children. I also hope to contribute to preventing a medicated society, and instead, a happy, informed and healthy growing population. I plan on having another child and seeing what inspiration and opportunities arise from that chapter of life, as I am already so grateful for the changes and openings having Jet has brought into our life.

I believe a huge factor to having a successful business when also being a mum, is doing something that you love and are passionate about.

For me, my learning and business growth has not only helped me on the career front, but also my family in the way of health and wellbeing. I did quickly realise that I was doing too much and giving too much of myself to areas that weren't important in the early years of my child's life, and hence tapered it back to just my own business. That way, I was able to set the boundaries of my limitations while still balancing being a mum and giving the deserved time to bringing up my son. As everyone says, 'you never get these years back' to which I 100% agree with from reflecting on the first fourteen months of Jet's life.

As mums, we have this need to still be someone outside of mum life, which we can, however we don't need to be more career woman than mum. Acknowledging the balance between the two is vital, and while I'm still in the baby years of mum-life, I do have bigger plans for my career once my children are in school. It has been a huge lesson for me to be okay with taking a step back in the meantime, letting my business cruise along without too much pushing or stress, and by knowing the time will come for it to pick up again, accompanying new opportunities that may just lead in a completely different direction.

Acceptance of the now, letting go of expectations and pressure, and trusting the future will deliver if I stay true to myself, are the three main things I remind myself regularly to get through these young years of motherhood and the career juggle.

Talita

Tracey Farrelly

Angels n Beyond

My children call me 'Mumma' and I'm Tracey to those who aren't my babies. Life has taken me on an amazing journey so far and I'm going to share some of this with you. Being a mum comes first, as it does for most of us. I also have a business I created called Angels n Beyond. I'm a Psychic Medium and owner of an online store, which has been developing and growing for over ten years. My gifts are mediumship, clairvoyance, clairsentience and clairaudience. My online store sells crystals, sterling silver and crystal jewellery.

I'm proud to say I'm a successful entrepreneur. Inspiring others with wisdom I have learnt, makes my heart sing. I'm also very passionate about many different charities. Over the years, to name a few: I've organised a clothing drive for domestic violence victims and raised funds for a Fiji school that had lost everything in a cyclone. They now have new tables, chairs and toys. Seeing them sitting at their new desks and singing for us gave me goosebumps.

I'm always striving to make a difference in peoples' lives. I'm blessed with two children, an eight-year old girl and a five-year old boy. I'm so proud of them both. Becoming a 'Mum' was a long time coming for me. That's a whole other story.

I know my actions will leave an imprint in my children's lives.

They're only young, but I often say, "you're never too young to learn to be compassionate and kind". They too can make a difference in many, many ways during their life. I devote my daily life to my loving husband, my gorgeous children and anyone else who needs my love or support. I inspire my children to be the best they can. I know I'm holding their hands for a short while, but their hearts forever.

I remember wondering what their voices would sound like. Hearing their first words followed what feels like shortly afterwards, their first words, then first sentences. I love listening to them counting to sleep as they're trying to learn their numbers; the overwhelming feeling of being so proud, you feel like you'll explode. This is what life is all about. Raising your babies to be confident and most importantly, encouraging them to be truly and genuinely *kind* people (no matter what others may do).

I'm blessed to be able to say I feel the excitement and sometimes pain of getting your little ones ready in the morning for school, guiding them with their reading, maths and story-telling. Feeling the absolute joy of cheering them on whilst on the sporting field. Then, there comes a time when you know you have still got more to give the world.

For many years, I went into an office environment daily. I worked for others, ensuring I gave my personal best, however I knew this wasn't my 'life's' contract' or passion to be in an office.

I'd sit and think, "I mustn't be the only one thinking there has to be more to life than this".

I've always been a positive spiritual person. One day I was sitting in the corporate world and I just knew this was not what I was meant to be doing with my life. I felt like the universe was constantly giving me signs and showing me there were other options for me out there; many different avenues for me to follow and also out there for anyone else who needed more in their life. So, I started to look at how I would like my own business to look. *What was I truly passionate about? How would I do this and make it a success? Which path should I take? What would feel like if I was doing what I loved?*

So, I created my own business. It began with Reiki and meditating, and through this, my psychic abilities opened up further. I then looked at ways to connect with spirit further and create different opportunities to help others develop their gift. Time flew, as did my connection to spirit. My online business was a natural progression to be a platform to share healing products on with the world.

Throughout the years, lack of time has caused many challenges and delays, however I pushed through these. Running our home, my business and being a mum constantly bring up new challenges daily. For example, ensuring all the washing is done when I've had thousands of entries to be put into my database. Ensuring my groceries are done and meals prepared, when I've had newsletters to write. Ensuring my housework was done, when I've had clients to call back and book in. This makes you realise we're all only human and there are really only twenty-four hours in a day.

I like to do things myself, so they're done the way I like them done. Some would say I'm a bit of a control freak! It is really hard sometimes to let go of things around the home - let alone things in your own business that you're constantly developing. Passing on the photography to my husband was a no brainer as that's one of his gifts. He's an amazing photographer. I knew he'd honour the business with the best photos. He's an extremely patient man and I've been blessed to have him understand. He's always been willing to contribute and support me to create my dream business by nurturing my own dreams. This has changed who I am and it's made me feel like a better wife and mum.

My children and I quite often sit with crystals and meditate. My son loves playing with crystals. My daughter loves dancing freestyle to meditation music with her Mumma. She also loves meditating with crystals. This is very healthy for our minds and bodies. We're living proof of how this enhances my children's and family's lives.

There are certain things in life you have to let go of. There are also certain things you have to let others help with if you can't do them yourself. This way, you can focus on your passion. Whatever you have decided you want to do to follow your dreams, make them a reality.

I believe I've attracted many amazing opportunities my way to expand my business over the years, such as appearing on Psychic TV which is aired worldwide, contributing to inspirational books published globally, and providing psychic readings at Mind, Body & Spirit Festivals across Australia. Doing regular readings with individuals and businesses has grown my own business around the globe. Connecting people with their deceased loved ones is truly a gift. Seeing what lies ahead for people and being able to guide them on the right path also is an amazing gift.

I'm honoured to say word of mouth is my advertising. I'm forever grateful to the souls I have met and am yet to meet. Through psychic medium readings, I'm able to help others find clarity in their life and heal by connecting with loved ones they've lost. Psychic medium readings just happened naturally for me. I did seek guidance from experts in this field to understand what it was I was seeing, feeling and hearing. Understanding how to interpret your visions is a whole other story, too. There are many, many courses you can attend to help with this. I strongly encourage others to develop and understand their gifts. There can never be enough people in this industry.

How I now give psychic readings is by connecting with your energy/spirit guides/angels by sitting opposite you across a table and connecting with you by holding your hands. I am a psychic, and my gifts include mediumship (seeing and hearing spirits who have passed over), clairvoyance (clear seeing), clairaudience (clear hearing) and clairsentience (clear presence). I still blow myself away at how this gift has gone from strength to strength and brings so much healing to others and myself. I truly believe everyone has the gift of being psychic; it's just that it is either shut down or nurtured when you are young. When I say shut down, I don't mean deliberately. I mean that some don't see the signs and know what little ones are doing when they say, "I'm talking to my friendly ghost" or "I saw Nanna last night in my room". If only everyone knew that in developing this gift, it could bring so much joy to themselves and those around them.

Reaching for your career change and finding your 'happy place' is not a long distance away, it is right there. Just recognising what it is you're passionate about and making it happen is the key.

Believe in yourself and your ability to think positively, be happy, have a light heart, make life changing decisions to do what makes your heart sing. Just remember this: it's a road which will flow easily if you're on the right path. If not, you will keep feeling like you're hitting road blocks. Stop, listen, and go back and have a look at what you're creating for yourself or your family. This usually means you should be going in a different direction to make it a success.

As mentioned before, who would have thought I'd be where I am today doing what I'm doing? Certainly not me! I used to laugh and say, "I can't meditate". As many women, men, mums and dads know, there is always something going on in our heads. However, with practice, I did. Whilst learning I'd be interrupted with thoughts popping into my head like, *I forgot to get milk*. I'd acknowledge the sentence, visualise the words float by, then dismiss it. I'd bring my mind back to the meditation music. There probably isn't a week that goes by now, that I don't share this guidance with a client.

Being a mum is what I ached for my whole life and earning an income that comes from loving what I do was what I hoped to achieve. My children know this is possible, now I've achieved it. It is still growing and growing day by day, minute by minute.

I knew I was healing my own life and by sharing my journey, I help others heal theirs or make their lives happier.

Sharing details of my journey with the world would is an honour. As a working mum, I've found my income through a place of peace for myself, my children and others. Believing you can and will be a success, is the first step to making your dreams a reality. My life has changed throughout the past decade dramatically. I wouldn't have it any other way, though. People often tell me, "I don't know how you do it". I completely understand this as I too, don't know half the time how I do it. However, how does any dedicated mum do what needs to be done to raise happy, content, kind little people?

Also, how many mums take a good hard look at themselves and think, "there must be more to life". Isn't being a mum enough? Well yes, it is - but being able to earn an income doing what you love day in day out and making it a business brings so much more into your life and the life of your children. Children really feel it when you're content. It also shows them that they too, can follow their dreams and create an income for themselves. An income doesn't always have to come from a corporate job or trade.

A mum living their dream and feeling at peace with who they are filters throughout the home and everyone who lives in it.

As a child, I was abused by the man who was meant to be my stepfather and give me a happy home. However, I was given the opposite. I held most of this trauma inside as I was too scared to express this verbally. From a young age, I learnt to pretend my world was a happy place. It was however as I said, the opposite. Inside was constant fear.

Fear that if I didn't pretend all was well in my world, there would be consequences. This also gave me the strength as I got older to know you *can* be a good mum and protect your children. You *can* give them that safe, happy place that I longed for.

All of my actions as an adult and especially since becoming a Mum myself, have been for my children. I am more than a Mum. I am a mum who has turned my past trauma into incredible strength. I was a fearful young girl/woman, and now a strong brave woman and mum.

I finally told my story publicly and went through the court process. This showed me just how strong and secure my life is now. I didn't feel this at the time, but I do now. It changed my life, my loved one's lives, and others too. I believe we have a journey already mapped out for us - we can't change the final outcome, we can only change how we get to the outcome. If its' been a rough road, then you may need to reach out to others to help lift you up or guide you in a different direction to reach true happiness in your life.

There is always someone out there who will listen and there is always someone out there who cares. You just need to be open to sharing and receiving.

My life and business have many exciting new opportunities constantly opening up to me and my family. I look forward to embracing them with open arms and an open heart.

Whatever it is that you think you want to do, and whatever it is that you think stands between you and that, stop making excuses. You can do anything.

-Katia Beauchamp, co-founder and CEO of Birchbox

Ruchika Rawat

Roo and Joey

My story starts in India, being born and brought up there, living a content life, in my own little bubble of happy existence. A well-established physiotherapist in the Department of Health and Family Welfare, married to a successful IT professional, working with an MNC, my life was headed exactly where I wanted. To add to this, my little bundle of joy - our daughter - arrived soon after, on 28th of March 2012. Life was good, and even though my husband had asked me about emigration a few times, I refused every time. I didn't even give it any thought, until that one day, that one incident that shook my country to its core- the Nirbhaya rape case, a physiotherapy intern gang raped and tortured in the heart of the capital city. Suddenly, my land didn't feel safe anymore.

Suddenly, the foundations that held me to my country - the security that cocooned me - were all broken in one big blow. How could I raise a daughter in a country where there was a molestation complaint every two hours, and a rape case every four hours? The mother in me couldn't fathom that the city that I grew up in was now so unsafe for my daughter, for all daughters, for women! That's when my husband and I decided to emigrate to Australia. Come 1st of January 2015, we reached Melbourne airport, and the memory is still fresh in my mind! How can I ever forget the words of the officer at arrivals who flipping the pages of my passport, asked, "Hey lady! Are you here for good?" I smiled and replied, "Yes, officer! For sure!" He responded with, "Welcome home". Wow! Nothing has inspired me or assuaged me like those two words, be it a low point or every victory that I achieve here; Australia is and always will be, home.

Starting from scratch in a new country is not easy. But, I am proud of our journey; enjoying, learning and evolving. From a family of three, now we are four. We have formed so many beautiful relationships! Melbourne is an astounding place - so very uniquely multicultural, and everyone is warm and cordial, like a cosmopolitan embrace.

Leaving my career as a physiotherapist after the birth of my son here, I ventured into entrepreneurship and started 'Roo and Joey', an online store for mums and bubs in May 2017. I have found that starting a business is one of the most exciting adventures that one can embark upon. My kids are my inspiration. I feel that being a mum has made me more creative and innovative as an entrepreneur. Be it multi-tasking, time management or having the ability to prioritise, being a Mumpreneur gives me an opportunity to work on what I am passionate about and interested in. Operating a home-based business gives me the flexibility to work and simultaneously take care of my children, and the added bonus of setting my own work schedule and being my own boss.

I launched Roo and Joey with a vision — "Blossoming Mums and Bubs!" The highlight of Roo and Joey is the eco fashion nappies and eco toilet training pants. I am passionate about the environment and I believe in sustainability to the core, from environment to social, to economic. Roo and Joey is not just an online retail store, it's more like a community built on these three pillars of sustainability; creating awareness and ever evolving. Our ethical and ecofriendly products are sourced from developing countries, providing economic support to families in the developing world. In terms of environment, Roo and Joey is leading the change for switching to cloth nappies for many multicultural families locally (at least partially, if not fully). And on the social front, it has been contributing to the cause of education for under-privileged children in third world countries by supporting various overseas non-profit groups and social activists.

I firmly believe in the greater good – giving back to the environment, to the community, and to my roots!

Gender equality and female empowerment is also very dear to me and I firmly feel the need for education and financial freedom for girls. That's why I also donate towards the education of under-privileged children in my home country. I have become part of the United Nations Women's National Committee Australia and want to carry further programs and projects. I have also become an advisor to the Women's Business School on diversity and inclusion for accelerator programs for women. This year I was among the top finalists for National Sustainability Award 2017 by the AusMumpreneur group.

Now, I am also working for a Vic Health project with the Alcohol and Drug Foundation for community research, primary prevention and awareness for CALD (Culturally and Linguistically Diverse) communities.

I am truly grateful for the life I am leading. It is everything and more that I envisioned my life to be like; a mix of everything - family, love, friendships, my tribes, hard work, determination, gratitude, contentment, happiness, success and most of all giving back; supporting one another and illuminating the world with our little efforts, putting gorgeous smiles on others' faces. The mum in me feels really proud when my five-year-old talks about donating her stuff to the needy or selling her artworks to buy toys for the kids who don't have any!

As Mahatma Gandhi rightly once said, "I am the change I want to see in the world". Also, I truly believe in the quote by William Jennings Bryan: "Destiny is not a matter of Chance. It is a matter of Choice. It is not a thing to be waited for. It is a thing to be achieved." And of course, the one quote that will always hold to be true, "Behind every successful woman is a tribe of other successful women who have her back".

My success notes for other women wondering whether they 'can':

- Go for it! If you believe in something, put your heart and soul into it.

- Have the right attitude. Be determined, stay focused, work hard and follow discipline (the most important).

- Remember, it is all about choices!

- Aspire to inspire.

- Believe you can and you will definitely succeed in whatever you do. Success is absolute, not relative. Believe in your uniqueness. That is your gift! That is your asset!

Ruchika

Laura McNally

Monkey Blue Press

I love a nice holiday. I mean, who doesn't? Sea, sand and sun, every girl loves a walk on the beach, sand between her toes the fresh sea air, but what I love most about a holiday is the airport. I love the busyness, the atmosphere, the voices and conversations between families, the smell of the fresh coffee. I love to sit and watch groups of girls with matching printed tops and flowers around their necks for that Hawaiian theme of a hen party they are returning from, giggling and laughing, reminiscing about the antics of the trip. The 'new' couple cuddled up together waiting for their flight number to be called, but so content and in love that it seems it wouldn't matter whether they reached their destination or not. The men loading their golf bags with excitement and clapping and rubbing their hands together with delight as they order their first round of beers at the bar. The tiny new born on her way home to be shown off to her grandparents for the first time, her parents fussing over her, wiping every single dribble to make sure she'll be immaculate upon pick up.

What I love most of all though, are the book shops in airports; the smell and the feel of all those new books. I remember being a young teenager on a school trip and having to be chased out of the book shops to continue the walk along with my twenty something classmates, but I knew some day, somehow, my book, with my name, would one day be placed on one of those shelves. Fast forward twenty years, and there they were. I proudly sat back and watched a shop assistant open a new box of books and out came a brightly coloured book, familiar characters popping out, connecting completely with me, so familiar, like I've seen them before, like I've known them all my life.

They were so familiar because they were mine and they're on a book that I created. A cover that belonged to me, a book to be proud of, and my name proudly stitched to each copy. As the member staff continued to unpack and stack, I allowed myself for just a brief moment to sit back and breathe in pure delight, before of course I rushed in to fix the positioning of the books, *my* books. Like any mum getting the last touch of their child's hair before they leave home, I repositioned them and gathered them together, so they were lined up and sitting straight. I removed the price sticker that was sloppily stuck in the centre and repositioned it to the top right-hand corner, Aaaahhh, there, that's better.

So, how did I get here? How did I go from having a children's book idea in my head to getting them stocked in the biggest bookstores in the world? Barnes and Noble, Amazon, Eason's and Waterstones, to name but a few. Well, it wasn't easy. I can start by telling you that. I am Laura Quinn, author and creator of Monkey Blue and Friends, founder and director of Monkey Blue Press.

This is my story, a story that now needs to be shared, a story that any working mum can relate to.

The first thing I said to my husband after an excruciating, long winded labour that inevitably ended up in a caesarean section was, "I'm never ever doing that again". The second thing I said? "There is no way on this earth I am returning to work." I felt it was my time now. I'd planned on staying at home and being a lady of leisure, Okay, I was slightly naïve, not to mention still high on pethidine. I'm not one for putting down other women, in fact I'm all about the women, but my reality of bringing home a baby verses the images I'd seen of Kate Middleton in her flowing dress, her blow-dried hair falling in to a wave like she just stepped out of a salon and not an actual maternity ward, well, let's just say, I fell short. I mean, it could have been me, it should have been me. I'd packed my dryer and straighteners, I'd mastered the art of the wavy blow-dry, I had the flowery dress from H&M and a makeup bag full of tricks. I had all the tools. The only difference was I neither had the energy to do it, nor the energy to care. I didn't even manage to brush my teeth and that wheel chair I'd foolishly snubbed in my way in, it became my very best friend on the way out. So, along with unwashed hair and teeth, an infected wound and the inability to walk, well it altered the image just a tad. My husband on the other hand, he mastered the 'William' in his crisp clean white shirt, so at least one of us succeeded.

I always had a passion for writing and was told I had a flare.

After getting back on my feet after having my son, I knew I just had an itch and regardless of my beautiful son and pending motherhood, I knew I wouldn't feel fulfilled until I got that itch and gave it an almighty scratch, which

I did. It was time for a major life overhaul, time to stop being afraid of making decisions, and time to focus on what I wanted. I had been going to writing conventions, workshops and clubs, hoping to meet with someone - anyone bedsides my parents and partner who critique with enthusiasm after reading three lines, bless them. I needed someone who would recognise my flare, love and passion for writing, and sometimes, as the age old saying goes, "It's not what you know, it's who you know". I thought I may have been too late. I don't have time to branch out now and meet and mingle to get the contacts I need. My hubby then called me to say that Karen McDermott from Serenity Press was coming to my local writer's club, Karen was our local 'urban legend'. I'd lived in a small town only a few miles from her where unfortunately there was very little on offer for us "arty farty" types, but she was the success story, the one that got away if you like, the girl that didn't sit talking or make excuses, but got out and just did it and I wanted to do the same.

I went to the talk and met with Karen and afterwards I relayed my rejections and disappointments to her - how every avenue was full of taking cuts and wanting percentages. I told her I was afraid in some cases to even share my book ideas. I was so confused and needed help. I told Karen I would submit some work, I did, and nervously waited on her response. I was delighted when she offered me a place in her new Making Magic Happen Academy. This academy is not only about the writing and perfecting it, it's not only about book sales, it is a complete insight and journey through the world of publishing. I was welcomed in to the academy on the 13th of June 2017. I knocked social events on the head, said goodbye to nights on the tiles with friends, and I set the wheels in motion. Any spare moment I had between doctor's appointments and birthday parties, I spent writing down my ideas. Sometimes I'd even have to pull over at the side of the road to take note of something that had come in to my head; a title or an ending maybe. I'd get a birthday party invitation and start cutting it up. When my husband raised his brows, I would smile in delight. "This is it," I'd claim, "this is the colour I want to use for the front cover". I'd wake up at 4am and run to switch on the computer in the spare room as a new character would pop in to my head and finally, before I knew it, I had my book.

I began my own publishing press, under the influence of my new mentor Karen. I called it Monkey Blue Press after the title of my first book and through it, I began the process of launching my first book of the Monkey Blue collection. The book itself is all about morals. My son was given a blue monkey as a gift and he loved it. I was documenting my son's actions and I was going to call the book curious Cian after him originally, but monkeys, well, they have much more appeal. I'd plan to discreetly add glasses of water to the pictures, and vegetables and fruit at every opportunity to encourage clean living and (I try) through the books to teach kids the importance of friendships and looking out for one another. I try to encourage kids to reach out of their comfort zones and make friends with people they might not have necessarily first thought they could be friends with. I love morals and as a writer of poems I love rhyme, so the book's content was easy and simply put together.

I then had the daunting task of trusting someone with my ideas, an artist who could bring Monkey Blue to life. I thought the illustration process would be a nightmare and I would have endless headaches, but instead of spending hours on the internet researching illustrators my local hairdresser suggested a local artist. My first thought was no, I want the book to be brilliant. Surely, I would need someone from London or the likes to create the book to my high expectations, but I took a peek at his work anyway. He had never illustrated a book before and was up for the challenge. He too was trying to venture in to the world of children's books, so we felt we had nothing to lose and together we got started. It was no doubt the most exciting part of the whole journey - I had a fabulous illustrator on board and we connected immediately; he saw my visions.

When I saw the first sketches, I knew he had taken everything I had said on board and I was internally grateful, but there were loads of ups and downs still to come along the journey to publication. My illustrator had created Monkey Blue exactly like I had envisioned, and the collaboration was a real success, there was no doubt about that. Monkey Blues Friends looked exactly how I had pictured, his work was fantastic and completely blew me away, the excitement was unreal as I waited for daily updates and sketches, once the colouring images came through I knew I had made the right decision and saved myself so much time and hassle as he just got it. It was like he was in my mind and knew exactly what I wanted. Needless to say, he created my second, and is now getting stuck in to my third book.

So, what next? The illustrations were under way, the book had been proof read and I wanted to press on. I was lucky to have Karen on hand 24/7 for guidance as the business does get complicated in so many ways - the uploading of files, the breaking down of images, the ISBN sourcing, the distribution, promoting and marketing. I was completely overwhelmed, but I took a step back and took a deep breath. I was already so invested that I had no other choice but to ride it out and continue, and I'm glad I did. I have a busy head and sometimes too many irons in the fire is not always a good thing. You end up all over the place and you become very unproductive in the end, so it's best to focus, take one thing at a time, deal with it and move on to the next thing. It's important to delegate at this point; with your home life also. Get your sister to take your kids for an hour while you type a cover letter, or let your parents take them for a sleepover while you attend a meeting with a stockist. I finally learned the art of delegating. It's hard. You obviously want to be in control of everything, but between the website, the promoting of the book, launches, events, my next book, invoicing, the diary for authors talks, and book readings, on top of my own appointments and my son's appointments, I just couldn't manage it all and I'm not ashamed of that.

I met with my local council and they loved what I was doing. They got behind my projects and have offered me much needed support; taking pressure off my outgoings with grants and aids for work on my website by an expert on their clock, advice and seminars to help with my networking and building my brand, and vouchers for a top accountant. They have helped me as much as they can and in turn, I have been interviewed by all the local papers.

When it comes to books, reviews matter, so I attended networking events and approached other ladies in business. While doing this, my illustrations were nearing completion and I had a contract with a local print house. The day I received my first proof copy was up there with other major events in my life, and it was the most exciting time! I was one proud lady. I took a little time to soak it in and I immediately began the process of posting out books to stockists and bloggers. I received raving reviews. One was from the Boots 2016 Parenting Blogger of the Year, One Yummy Mummy, and the second from an extremely popular group of writing experts who all happen to be ladies and mums from a magazine and website called the F Word, a blog that receives thousands of views a week. Everyone was getting behind me and Monkey Blue and it felt amazing. I was now officially an author.

The next time I had to fill out a survey or a form for the bank, I could use that as my occupation, an *author*.

So, running Monkey Blue Press, this entailed creating my own personal Ingram Spark account where I first upload the cover and files of the book (not my forte), but with help from Karen, I got there. I can personally run daily sales reports and have complete control over my books and the advertising, as well as a complete over view of sales in each country around the world. It's literally cutting out the middle man and minding my own business; being the first to see sales figures, making calls on behalf of myself and getting the details first. I am due to do my first author's talk at a women's enterprise event and I have booked talks in schools, as well as readings of the books at all sorts of events. I created my own website for my press and book collection, and a place for people to follow my story. I have now confidently approached outside distributors and major book stores with submissions, and alas, had them accepted, and boy it feels good. The scene in the Pretty Woman movie comes to mind when Julia Roberts returns to the lady who first snubbed her in the clothes shop: "Big mistake, I mean big, huge!" I too, have that feeling. I was going to get there regardless of who was going to support me, and I did. I want to let you all know that following your dreams and making them a reality is indeed possible. Just peek at the cover of Monkey Blue and as hard as it is to believe now, this was just once a dream – an image I had in my head – but is now a reality.

This is my new reality and it feels great. It can be yours as well. A lot of hard work? Yes. Time consuming? Yes. But, worth it? A big yes! This collection is not only my first book as an author, but the first book I published as a publishing press. My aim was to have the big stores stocking the book and just like anyone who Googles themselves, I sneak on at night and breathe in with pure delight when I see it stocked on Amazon and Barnes and Noble. I check in on it, too. Like the first nights of taking home a new born, I would wake in the middle of the night and look in his cot to make sure he was still breathing. I do the same with Monkey Blue. I check the Waterstones website, time after time, night after night, just to make sure it's still there, it hasn't been removed, it hasn't been replaced, I sigh and breathe in, *Oh, thank god it's still there.*

Monkey Blue is on some of the biggest and best platforms I could personally wish for and I watch nervously as the books filter down in to the right channels and distribution companies. The buzz and excitement are something else altogether. Waterstones are what I would call the crème of the crème of book stores - they don't accept anything but the best - so much so that you have to go through so many channels just to talk to a buyer; never mind actually getting them to take it. But, as of now, the book is up there, and I am so proud of that. Should it all end now, I can say I am at peace and I have achieved what I wanted. It was my end goal.

I am delighted that my second book collection, 'What on Earth is under my Bed?' has now also been published. This is a Halloween book I plan to produce every year with a different twist each time. I am currently arranging more book launches for this book. My first big one was in my local Eason's store and it was a fabulous morning. Eason's is a massive chain in the UK and again, this book is being stocked by Amazon and Barnes and Noble, and some of the bigger stores as well.

We all must start from somewhere, and I'm so glad I gave myself that extra nudge to push on and achieve the goals I set for the business and for myself, personally.

It has been such an amazing and exciting time. When I saw the first cover of Monkey Blue, I was ecstatic. As wrong as this may sound to some, it was almost up there with seeing my son for the first time. I already felt like I had succeeded. Ironically, it was also a long labour of love, but most certainly one I would do repeatedly. I would love to inspire any other mums out there that want to follow their dreams not to feel as though they're being selfish or more to the point, judged. The stars are up there, and they *are* in reach. I used whatever ladders, scaffolds and shoulders I needed, but, I got there. I took mine and there's still loads left up there. My life has changed dramatically since the birth of my son, as from that, came the birth of Monkey Blue and Friends. I have help now with my son, so that I can work during the day and attend whatever events I need to in the evening time.

Networking is a massive part of growing any business and is essential in the growth of your own profile. I am not the most confident of people socially, so I needed some coaching in public speaking as I find I am doing that quite regularly now. Once upon a time I would have stared blankly at one person to focus on in a talk. I know I need to engage better with groups of people, so I am still learning and developing as a business person, and there is always loads to learn along the way. I love the thought of my books being out there, I do. They are in the big bad world, probably getting scribbled over by some kid with a crayon, but they are out there, and I am out there. My only regret is that I didn't believe in myself a little bit earlier.

Laura

We need to do a better job of putting ourselves higher on our own 'to do' list.

-**Michelle Obama**

Anu Sawhney

Bidiliia

My name is Anu, short for Anuradha. It is a challenging name to pronounce, hence the short form. I am the owner and designer of Bidiliia - an atelier based in Sydney, Australia that honours the craftsmanship of ethically handcrafted fashion jewellery.

As all small business entrepreneurs know, that is only the official introduction. In real life, we have many more job titles - accountant, business manager, publicist and marketing manager. Also, secretary, coffee bringer, inventory manager, technical support, HR manager and sometimes, janitor. For me, however, it all starts with being a Mum to a kind, generous and curious four-year-old young lady who inspires me each day to be a better person.

I would like to take this opportunity to provide an insight into my journey, my achievements and struggles, and how I became a mumpreneur. I do this in the hope that reading about my journey from the depths of despair to an aspiring, normal-ish parent and entrepreneur may inspire another mum who's a small business owner or aspirant to take the leap, follow their dreams and become a source of strength, love and joy.

I was born in India in 1980 to a family of armed service members. My mother was the outlier in the family - trained in interior design, she chose to strive out as an independent designer undertaking design-build projects on her own. This is significant to my story because in the eighties, Indian women were still confined to the home. To step out of the home to work, that too as an independent designer, dealing with largely uneducated male contractors and workmen was a feat in itself. To say that her work was challenging is putting it mildly. To work as an entrepreneur is hard anyway. To break social norms, rub shoulders with men, command the respect of men who worked under her while they did not allow their wives and daughters to even be literate... that is nothing short of an Olympic feat.

My mother has always been an inspiration to me. Not just for the reasons mentioned above, but also because while she was shattering norms and breaking glass ceilings, she strove for an unparalleled perfection in her actual work. I inherited this strong spirit of charting my own course despite odds, a good design sense, rock solid ethics and acute business skills. I also inherited the inside scoop on how running your own business can be so exciting and incredibly empowering, but it comprised of blood, sweat and oceans of tears.

In 1998 I commenced a four-year Fashion Design degree at the National Institute of Fashion Technology (NIFT), Mumbai. Now NIFT is rated as one of the top twenty design schools in the world, but then it was the only option available to us in India. I met my now husband Vinit, while I was still studying. After graduating in 2001, I worked with some local fashion houses and in 2006, Vinit and I got married just before he was sent to Sydney for work. That is how I ended up in Sydney, Australia, which has been my home for the last eleven years. Starting over in a new country is hard, but I was determined, and after a few years of struggling, I found work with some of the more well-known design and buying houses.

I thought I would have the usual life and career track – keep working, have a family, and live happily ever after.

I used to often toy with the idea of going solo and starting my own design workshop and manufacture something. I played with the idea of creating artwork, home furnishings and jewellery. Each avenue was exciting and interesting. I have the ability to create exceptional products in each, but for one reason or another, or perhaps due to sheer lack of momentum, the solo flight kept getting deprioritised.

In 2008, I was diagnosed with Rheumatoid Arthritis of the degenerative type. It is an auto-immune condition where in due course, one's joints fuse together due to excess calcification, resulting in total loss of mobility. I was faced with the reality that one day I may be fully disabled. A bit scared, I plunged head first into traditional treatments - non-steroidal anti-inflammatory meds et al. Initially my body responded to these, but soon it sunk in that these treatments were not sustainable long term as they cause more harm than benefit.

I started looking at alternative medicine and my research took me to various parts of the world. I started a regimen on managing my disease and condition through herbal supplements and alternative therapies involving annual trips to India. I was still working full time, and even though this felt like a tremendous personal setback, my love for design helped me look forward, knowing that I carried this secret burden daily, vowing to never let it crush my spirit. Living with RA was painful - both physically and emotionally – on a daily basis. On rainy days the pain was unbearable, and yet in design I found relief and joy - an escape from my body that was slowly fusing and becoming immovable. It was in this 'pain bearing space' that I shaped up what would become Bidiliia; where I learnt to be more forgiving, less judgemental and a little bit more Zen about what was happening to me.

My husband and I also really wanted children, and while this health condition was taking over our lives, we decided to give it an honest try because my body may not cooperate as time went by. Thankfully the pregnancy itself was viable and joyous, and we were blessed with our daughter.

But, the hormonal changes post pregnancy accelerated the RA degenerative process and by the time my baby was only four months old, my hip joints had totally fused, and both my knees were well on their way to irreversible damage! I was in pain, so much pain that the pregnancy, C-section and recovery pales by comparison to the physical pain of caring for a baby while being disabled. It is also nothing compared to the mental pain of seeing your life fall apart before your eyes because you know that you will never really be able to live a regular life. I had no extended family or friends to help, and my partner tried his best while working full time. I tried to end this existence several times during that period.

In these darkest of times, when I did find joy, it was looking at my daughter, but also in those faint moments when we went stepped out of the apartment as a family to go for a drive or grab dinner. Those times, I would make the effort to change out of pyjamas and pull out a well-crafted piece of art to wear. That piece of design, that jewellery started meaning more than an accessory to me. It became an anchor of normalcy, of making me feel like ME, when other parts of me no longer did. The pieces reminded me of why I bought them, when I bought them. The story behind the craft, the places I searched and the part of world I bought it from and occasion I bought it for. I held on to those moments because they showed me what I had lost and where I longed to go back again.

It was in 2015 that as a family we decided that I should go ahead with bilateral full hip replacement surgery, followed closely by a total knee replacement surgery. The preparation for the surgery was difficult, but I was immensely hopeful. Due to my age, the scope of success and full rehabilitation was high. I had already decided on jewellery being my main theme. But, I was looking to make a difference. Between numerous tests and doctor's visits, there was a lot of time I spent waiting. Instead of waiting, I started channelling that time reading up on craft practices, the industry, and the decline in craftsmanship at the hands of disposable fast fashion and unethical practices.

In waiting rooms and between blood tests and scans, my business vision and philosophy started to take shape. While admitted in the hospital I started drawing, and during my rehab stint, I finalised the first designs. Soon after I came home, I started the manufacturing process and finalising the brand details, and the gears to get it off the ground.

This business would be my contribution to slow, sustainable, scalable fashion jewellery.

My jewellery would come from a place of honesty and love – because I cared more about who makes the jewellery than how much the jewellery makes for me. I wanted this business to have the ability to pick someone up when they were feeling down; to rescue someone who needed an anchor; to make someone feel awesome when they were not feeling so awesome. This business would be my attempt at giving back the craft of exceptional handcrafted fashion jewellery, bringing them back into the hands of artisans that have the experience and knowledge. It would be distinguished and limited edition. But above all, it would be ethical, spectacularly handcrafted jewellery. For everyone.

This business was born out of my tears for the sake of those that I loved – like my daughter, so it would be named appropriately. I named it Bidiliia because it is a derivation of my daughter's name and means strength and power. The product arrived, I took pictures and finalised my website. I decided that the right time was NOW, so in a post-surgery 'now or never' moment, I removed the password protection on my website on a lovely August afternoon, and Bidiliia was set free.

Having seen my mum running her business, I thought I had seen it all. I thought I was well prepared because I knew the drastic highs and lows of a family business and how it affects the dynamic and relationships within a family. I thought the most important parts of running a design business were to convert designs into reality, to honour and respect those who create for you, and the ethics of always taking the full turn and not cutting corners. I thought the most important skill was one I already had - of always making good on a promise - to clients and to the artisans. How wrong I was!

Nowadays, above all, one needs very savvy marketing skills to stay afloat. I was naïve to think that a great concept and product is ALL you need to run a successful business. Looking back, I think I should have spent more time focusing outward on social media and marketing. I would probably have spent more energy on crafting pre-launch jargons and on strategies to build anticipation in the marketplace. Since I arrived at this point from another route, I have had to play catch up after I launched. After putting in a lot of sleepless nights, I think I finally have an approach to working social media networks that I am comfortable with, funnels (yup, that's a thing!), opt-ins and an overall more holistic marketing strategy.

When I find myself getting overwhelmed, going back to why I started Bidiliia helps me find my centre - the ability to be an anchor, the core ethics of my business, respect for the craft and artisans, and bridging the gap between exceptional quality and affordability.

Being a mumpreneur has also taught me that work-life balance is a basic necessity and needs constant vigilance. I have to be watchful for times when I could really squeeze in an extra twenty minutes of work, versus being a parent. Making that choice means for a richer life, but also means working more midnight shifts to give work the attention and traction it needs. As much as I want to be a good parent and give my child the attention she needs, I am also a parent to the newborn Bidiliia. It needs to be nourished and watched so that it can stay staunchly true to its core principles and remains a conscientious business.

Even after eleven years, Australia is not home ground for me. Even though I have many friends and lots of great acquaintances, there is a lack of family support network that I can blindly rely on. As one matures and has children and delves deeper into work, one finds that friendships are harder to maintain. To complicate matters for me, I had the additional barrier of being ill and out of circulation that keeping up with people became challenging for me. Thus, for the better part, I have had to rely on myself and only do whatever I can manage with the support of my little family. For feedback, and outside opinion, I do reach out to anyone and everyone. And for professional hurdles, I signal to my network of past and present colleagues.

Not having a strong network of family support may not be an ideal situation, and if any mumpreneur has that, then it is a huge advantage. What seemed to be a barrier in the lack of support instead, was a gift that made me so incredibly discerning on how much to take on and saved me from overloading myself or wasting time with fruitless activities.

I am very hopeful about the future because I have my family and Bidiliia. The time where I was near fully disabled and needed help even to use the bathroom will stay with me the whole time. Having the opportunity to go through life restoring surgery and rehabilitation, I am very optimistic and raring to shape my future. I would like my story, the story of Bidiliia to be an inspiration to other women who might be facing adversity and need a ray of hope. Having a life changing experience puts fear of the next step and fear of failure in perspective. We only live once. Either we can live in fear, in anticipation or a limbo space between the two. Or, we can just decide that life is for living and start taking small significant steps. The most important thing to remember is that we must be true to our principles and try to do good in the world outside.

The journey of being an entrepreneur and putting your heart on the line is not easy. Being a mumpreneur is even harder because you are juggling two little babies, essentially. And just like with kids, there will be days where nothing will seem to work. On those days, divert your attention and focus on the passion that led you down this path in the first place. Whatever you do and whenever you start running and owning your own business, be honest and do it with all your heart. Do not leave your desires to whim and work at them one micro step at a time. Be ready to fail and fall. And when you fail and fall, get back up again and dust yourself off. Remember that in family we find strength and love, and in work we find joy.

Bidiliia is an anchor that brought me out of my depths. It is also a beacon of hope for the future. And while it takes baby steps towards the future, it is an acute reminder of the impact we can choose to have on the world. For me, Bidiliia is a reminder that daily, I choose strength to keep going, love for all around, and joy that I choose to feel within myself and share with the world.

Claire Orange

BEST Programs 4 Kids

> Strength through adversity. The strongest steel is forged by the fires of hell. It is pounded and struck repeatedly before it's plunged back into the molten fire. The fire gives it power and flexibility, and the blows give it strength. Those two things make the metal pliable and able to withstand every battle it's called upon to fight.
> **Sherrilyn Kenyon**

It was almost as if that was written for and about me as a woman — and a mum, in business. And I know that I am not alone on the journey — that being a mum in business is all about being resilient and resourceful, about finding a way even when the will is flagging, about doing more, giving more and being more even when there is nothing left in the tank. Then going to bed and doing it all over again the next day.

I am the co-director of BEST Programs 4 Kids co-founded with Helen Davidson. It is an international company with the mission to change the lives and outcomes of children everywhere. A company that has been forged and molded by the collective professional, personal and business learnings of two directors - both of us women, and both of us having raised children whilst working and juggling those complex and competing demands. Our company provides resources and training for children, parents, teachers and health professionals all over the world, and we focus on the skills at the heart of every successful, resilient and flourishing child and family. These skills involve the development of emotional intelligence and social competence through strong relationships with self and with others, the banking of resilience against a lifetime of ups and downs - because they're inevitable.

Reaching the point of running a business with my heart at the centre wasn't somewhere I got straight away. As with most women who run their own business, there seems to be a litany of attempts - some successful and others nothing short of horrendous - to get to the point of running *the* business - the one that brings together all of the skills and all of the learning from everything that's come before. It's fair to say that I've had a few bites of the 'business apple' in trying to get to the point of wider scale influence and internationally available resources.

Twenty-five years ago, I started my professional life as a Speech Pathologist working in the health system. I had two enormous learnings come out of the various roles I worked in in those early years. The first learning was about myself and my issues with working within a rigid system that often made no sense to me at all. Working within the established rules of an organisation where flexibility, innovation and creativity had no place was stifling for my entrepreneurial spirit. The second learning was about the children and families with whom I worked. In this time, long before the advent of my own family, I learned about the complexities of juggling the competing demands of being an adult and raising a child - or children.

Those learnings became a point of fascination and curiosity - a compelling journey to understand the heart of the child and their family and what made them tick - or not. So, despite having a series of fantastic and challenging positions in my early career days, I started reading about an area of children's mental health called Social and Emotional Learning. Even though I didn't know it then, my pathway to BEST Programs 4 Kids was being laid.

Cue the commencement of my own family. Four little boys were welcomed over seven years and there was enormous learning for me over this time — of course about the craft of motherhood, but also about myself and what I really wanted. I was torn, as many women are, with the desire to be there for every moment of my children's growing up whilst continuing to develop myself professionally and stimulate myself intellectually. So, I set about a process of self-reinvention — combining what I knew with where I wanted to go, and all of this around the constant demand of mothering four children.

My first business was launched, and I was sure that it was going to be the answer to being available for my children and pursuing my interest in child and family wellbeing.

This was a business I started with a school friend - a three-year-old kindy with a specialist language unit attached. It grew and grew from two half-days to two full time centres. Let me back-track to the bit about opening a business with a friend. This was my greatest learning from this experience, other than the fact that making money is much harder than it seems. Together we grew the business, however, things got messy, the friendship dissolved and that impacted our ability to continue running the business together. I bought out her share, but it wasn't the same and within a couple of years I sold the business.

Sometimes, as it seems to happen, learnings about self and life come in strange and unexpected ways. With four little boys in tow, my husband and I moved to the United Kingdom for two years — to explore, to reset and to experience life differently for a while. There was no time to run any business during this time as due to no school places being available, I educated my four boys from home. Through this experience, what was initially a point of fascination and curiosity, became compelling - a mission. I wanted to know more - in fact, everything I could about a child's ability to reach their potential and to flourish. What were the key factors? Intelligence, access to resources, top level education with all of the bells and whistles? In those two years I came to the beautiful realisation about the growing, shaping and influencing of successful children. That successful and fulfilling friendships were a driving force for children. That attitudes and behaviours in learning trumped everything - even intelligence. That the three loudly proclaimed 'R's' of reading, writing and arithmetic were nowhere near as important as the other R's — relationships and resilience.

On returning to Perth due to a harrowing, chronic illness experienced by my eldest son, I knew I had little capacity to engage in work requiring an outpouring of care, compassion and connection - all of that had to be held in reserve for my family. But, the drive to be productive and contribute saw me starting another business - nothing to do with any established skillset - of all things, I sold environmentally aware stationery to schools. Yes, recycled pencils, pens and papers. Again, the learnings were twofold. Firstly, selling product in an already crowded market is tough, exhausting and soul-destroying. Secondly, if you don't work from passion then it really is work, and who wants to do that? I love the saying, "Do what you love, and you'll never work a day in your life."

You may be wondering why I've shared my checkered path through the world of business - that litany of successes and failures that have the power to bring you to your knees? I reflect often on that path too at times, and with the great benefit of hindsight what I do know is that each and every one of those experiences laid the path to BEST Programs 4 Kids. There is no experience in that array that I could have done without to be where I am now. In business, failure at some point is a given. There have been many times I have been so bone-weary, so emotionally exhausted, so deeply depleted that I wanted nothing more than to go back to bed and hide under the covers. I have doubted myself, my ability and my commitment. I haven't backed myself and I've played small. But I know that I am the strongest steel, that there have been many fires that have forged me into the shape I am, and I know that there are many to come. And that's quite okay, because all of those experiences and learnings collectively are what I use to drive me passionately forward.

Which brings me to BEST Programs 4 Kids and what it stands for: an accumulation of many years of professional experience, personal learnings and a deep longing to be an agent for change. Fortuitously, an amazing woman had been on a similar journey and was also at the point of longing to translate her knowledge into a resource that would transcend the time limitations within her own clinical practice. The stars aligned, and I met Helen Davidson – my business partner and friend. We planned, talked, schemed and reminisced on our many and often outlandish group therapy experiences and eventually we put pen to paper and wrote a primary school resource that we called Highway Heroes. Using the metaphor of travelling along The Highway of Life, we wrote a curriculum that helps children to identify and manage the many social, emotional and learning BUMPS and HAZARDS (little and big adversities) that they have and will experience. The Highway Heroes curriculum is one that we wrote to help every child to manage the important stuff of childhood - the stuff that will shape their adult lives. Knowing and managing their own emotions, making and keeping friends, sorting out the tough stuff that happens in friendships, managing teasing and bullying, and developing their learning to learn skills.

There is a question I ask often and have asked all over the world: what are your top three skills and attitudes that make you successful in your career? Fascinatingly, this question is always met with the same responses: empathy, rapport, communication, negotiation, leadership, relationships, the ability to get along, assertiveness, responsible decision-making, self-control, persistence, confidence, resilience, self-acceptance. These are the skills that define Social and Emotional Learning — skills common to all children and adults, skills that are sewn in the formative childhood years.

Since the inception of BEST Programs 4 Kids my life has changed, and I know that it will continue to change at an exciting and alarming rate. The running of my own business has meant many sacrifices - made by me, my children, my ever-devoted husband and my family. Travelling for speaking, training and media opportunities has meant that I have been absent for days and occasionally even weeks. And those that love me and support my incredible yearning for better outcomes for every child have stepped in to fill the void my sporadic absence has created. As part of developing the business — actually, let me step out from behind that shield and just be deeply truthful, as part of developing *myself*, I have taken on roles and responsibilities that were not part of the original conceptualisation of the business.

It is my drive, my passion and the song of every cell of my being that every child - all of my own included - has access to support, resources and people who will hold them up, help them and be the soft place to land when life gets tough.

Now, that has meant having to step into roles that stretch my courage and commitment to the limit. Being called an 'expert' is a heavy responsibility and having to be that on live TV and radio cranks it up to another level. In fact, it has caused consternation in my internal world - I often walk the well-worn path of the self-doubter, the self-criticiser and I am by far my own harshest judge. It might seem strange to those external to my own world of self-judgement that I often doubt being good enough, knowing enough, being smart or refined enough to walk in some of the circles that I do. And I think that many women walk this well-worn path and that I am not alone - that if I look around, there would be many walking beside me wondering if they too were going to be found out or found lacking.

Challenges - of the many involved in the world of small business, surely, this has to be of the most significant. The challenge to rise above one's own self-judgement and to achieve - if only to prove that self-judgement wrong. Since childhood I have had high expectations of myself - I think it is referred to by many as perfectionism and I raise my hand and acknowledge that for many years, my best was simply not good enough - for me. Now, as I challenge myself to do better, be better and achieve more, it is no longer about proving to myself that I am good enough - it is about changing the world one child at a time. Imposter Syndrome nips at my heels from time to time - I don't think any high achieving woman is able to dodge the bullet of this. The teeth can bite and sting and slow me to the point of stagnation as I worry about whether I really am good enough, I am enough and whether I have what it takes to surpass my own expectations. And, of course, when Imposter Syndrome is a visitor in my often-complicated headspace, I do what we all do and find evidence to prove it right.

Earlier this year, for example, I was sitting alone in a studio waiting for my very first live television interview - one of many that now form part of the fabric of my week. It was the first though and I was a bundle of nerves, which completely made me forget to ask where to look for the cameras. Oh no! During the interview there were perhaps two minutes in which I managed to look at the camera and the rest of the time, well, you can imagine what that looked like. Of course, I went to town on myself. Not cut out for it. Leave it to the professionals. Eroded my professional credibility and my knowledge base. Sleepless night! Thankfully, my dogged, stubborn persistence to never lay down and give up kicked in and I fronted up the next week and the next, each time learning a little more until now - when the camera rolls and I sit in my happy space, knowing and believing that my words in a few minutes might just get to the right ears. Just one family, one parent, one child - and that's enough to make it all worthwhile.

But, there are other challenges. There is the constant jostling for prime space and position in the marketplace. We are not alone out there, peddling wares in the Social and Emotional Learning space - far from it. We compete with programs who have been out there longer and who have national recognition. In the age of 'evidence-based', a collective fifty-five years of experience seems not to be enough for some, despite Highway Heroes being a resource approved by the Australian Psychological Society. But, the moment those emails arrive that tell us that a child has behaved differently, that a child's life has changed, that a family have turned a corner - that makes it all worthwhile and makes us hungry for more.

Any business competing in the noise to be heard needs to get creative in their thinking, to be brave and to make courageous moves that are not always comfortable.

Being seen as a person of influence is assisted, most greatly, by a presence in the media. This is a relatively new way of thinking for me and it's taken time, effort and energy to develop relationships, to show up time and time again even when juggling other commitments becomes like an Olympic event. However, nothing has greater reach, greater promise of adding credibility and visibility - so for any business wanting to get their nose out in front of the pack, it's a unique way to get noticed and to influence many lives and opinions at once.

Then, there's the challenge of being everything within the business. Running the social media - so that it is meaningful and value-adds to the life of our online community, managing the accounts, feeding the hungry mouths of staff - even in the lean times, writing resources, keeping up-to-date with research and staying current in the media - it's a machine that needs feeding and nurturing — day in, day out, in sickness and in health - yes, much like a marriage. Meeting that challenge again requires creativity and courage. Entrusting the running of some aspects of the business into the hands of others leaves space to do what you're really good at. Being absolutely militant with your time is essential - time for tasks, lists to tick off and people to delegate to. Essential aspects of running a business - all of which require their own time to get up and running.

Let's not even talk about prioritising tasks as an entrepreneur. Every prospect seems exciting and inviting, there is so much to do, learn and know and then to translate into resources, products and training to allow others access to that know-how too. It's an enormous challenge separating the wheat from the chaff. Enormous! And this is where a great mentor, an external auditor of your thoughts and wild excitements is vital. That steady someone who can listen patiently, nod along silently and then come in with the cold hard truth of whether it's going to make money, whether it's a priority, whether it's possible. You'll know this person as they're the one you want to throttle most often - until you settle back and think over their wisdom and loathingly agree that they're mostly likely right and that prioritising is a good idea - even if a little staid and boring for a rampaging entrepreneur.

The greatest challenge - making money. Why is it so hard to make the stuff that makes the world go around? It's especially difficult when for some it seems to be an overnight achievement and for you it's a slow and steady climb. With my feet dragging, my shoulders slumped and an enormous sigh of resignation for having to plan well ahead in infinitely boring detail, I have come to the great realisation that a business plan is indeed, a necessary tool for growing a successful business. Anyone like me will know my pain in having to plan well ahead, make projections, have a content marketing plan – and then stick to it. Only enough room for a little bit of wildly extravagant movement, uninhibited thinking, planning and scheming. But, it is the way towards success for most of us and a good learning after many years of brilliant ideas without a care for a plan.

What I know about challenges – because there have been many of the course of my personal and business life – is that they build capacity – "Strength through adversity". Looking for the opportunity in each and every challenge changes your mindset and your focus and helps you to lift your eyes from the messy and demanding here and now to the prize on the horizon. As a Mum in business, I value the input, expertise and the loving support of those around me – family, friends, colleagues and associates. There is a poignant saying, "No (wo)man is an island," and there is enormous strength in being able to lean on those who want you to succeed.

Without the support of my family and extended family, pursuing my mission would be an impossibility. I am grateful eternally for the unconditional support of my husband – a man who has believed in me even when I had no self-belief left. A man who has and does go a million miles and who always, *always* has my back. And then there's my family who love and support me, who help with the endless array of activities that every family has to orchestrate on a daily basis so that every child gets where they need to go when they need to be there. It is support that I don't take for granted and I'm very conscious of hoping that I, in turn, give as much as I receive – which I do believe to be fundamental to a robust economy of giving and receiving in a family and community.

As only an ethnic child would understand, one whose family has left their country of origin to take up residence in another for the express purpose of giving their children the very best start in life, the deep, deep desire to prove that the sacrifices were worthwhile is ever-present. For me, it is part of my pleasure and measure of success that the difficulties my parents shouldered in silence in leaving their home, their country and their families is honoured by the success I chase, crave and achieve.

As a woman in business, it is often the strength and fortitude of other women I look to for courage and inspiration. Those who have trodden the path before me and overcome all manner of obstacles. It is a peculiarity that in business as a woman and a Mum, it is often other women and Mums who can be the least supportive, women who call you a friend but, perhaps, have different feelings about you being successful in the world of business. It's essential to culture relationships outside of those friendships that you can draw on for strength and inspiration. I have the great honour of calling on the support of particular women in my tribe and it is given generously and unreservedly.

Through the many and varied experiences that have shaped my understanding of business, the need to have an outcome in mind, the need to make decisions that are not always popular or easy and the need to carve out a niche in the marketplace are best supported by those with the same way of thinking, the same priorities and the same ability to give the business life. A business partner is an essential part of the success of a business and for me, I have always entered the world of business with a partner - not for any particular reason other than that person being as enthusiastic and as driven as I to achieve the intended outcome of the business activity. This working relationship needs to transcend friendship and rise into the highest forms of non-verbal communication; trust, loyalty, honestly and integrity. To be inspired by the journey, the many adversities, the unwavering spirit and the dogged determination of another is surely the greatest gift in partnering someone along the very bumpy road of running a business and being an entrepreneur. Helen and I planted a seed, we watered it, watched it germinate and now it's growing and blooming. Together we have made huge decisions - some easy and some painful but we work together to achieve our mission - which we put out the front of all of endeavours and efforts.

Building a business tribe is essential. The strongest and most courageous women that I model myself on are all those that give generously, laugh off their failures and get back up and have another go. They're all women who have, like steel, been dipped in the fires of life many times and have been forged into strong, resilient, outstanding women.

Let me look to the future - where I'm going and how I'm getting there. The mission of BEST Programs 4 Kids is to positively impact and change the lives of as many children, their families and communities as possible. Planning for growth in the next five years means even wider exposure - and of course the media is a given in this equation. So, that is one of my firm goals - to grow my presence as an influencer and educator - which means keeping on top of reading, keeping on top of research and keeping on top of being in the right place at the right time. The business can only grow if we add people skilled to do the many time-consuming jobs that encroach on creative and innovation time and despite the risks associated with this, it is a factor that requires thought and planning - and probably many attempts to get right. And then there are those pipe-dreams, the ones I nurse and bring out occasionally to turn over with anticipation. A TED Talk, commencing my PhD, international speaking opportunities - they're all in the pipe-line waiting for their turn in the sunshine. Actually, waiting for some available time and energy - which means that they will be nursed for quite some time.

Finally, I'd like to share some words of wisdom. Be flexible - it is almost a given that whatever you have planned will not turn out the way you envisaged. Be courageous - take some measured risks. Back yourself - sometimes you may well be the only one who does. Silence the doubters - in whatever way because they have the potential to become your inner voice. Have a plan - always have a goal out the front of you to direct your efforts towards. Don't be afraid to make money – an often-difficult obstacle for women in business where the focus is on helping rather than financial reward. Know where to draw the line on altruism - you are valuable, your time is valuable. Dream big - why not? Write down those dreams that you're too afraid to share with others and then find ways to make them come true.

As women – Mums - in business, every crazy moment in every crazy day seems to have to be carefully planned, mapped and prioritised. There are days where I am not sure how I will get everything on my 'Things to do' list accomplished - and sometimes I do and other times I don't. So, I do the best I can with the resources I have available, I rest and then I repeat and slowly, slowly I make a difference.

Claire

Whatever you do, be different — that was the advice my mother gave me, and I can't think of better advice for an entrepreneur. If you're different, you will stand out.

-Anita Roddick, founder of The Body Shop

Emma Lovell

CoziGo – Sleep on the Go

I'm Emma – wife to Phil, mum to Aimee and Harry, and owner of CoziGo – Sleep on the Go. Originally from the UK, I have made the beautiful Northern Beaches of Sydney, Australia my home for the last eighteen years. I came to Australia as a twenty-something backpacker and quickly decided that I loved everything this sunburnt land had to offer.

The plan to stay three months soon developed in to a more long-term plan (much to my mum's devastation) but even she found it hard to argue with me as I settled in to the 'daily grind' of being a Climb Leader on the Sydney Harbour Bridge. It was one of the most exciting jobs I've ever had and in Winter when their business was slower, I'd take three months off to be a Contiki Tour Guide and travelled around Australia, New Zealand and Fiji. Tough hey?

Eventually, I had to admit to myself that this kind of work was not paying the bills... well not at least, if I wanted to drive a car or not have six flat mates! I toyed with the idea of going back to teach at high school but wanted to explore business further. I had a few jobs that saw me managing other people's businesses and helping them with start-ups. I learned that I loved to be a part of journeys from the very beginning. There's nothing more exciting than seeing something come from nothing, so I became somewhat of a 'start-up specialist'. The last 'proper' job I had was as part of the start-up team at Q-Station Retreat. I was part of the team that was responsible for changing the National Park that was once a Quarantine Station into a 4.5 Star accommodation retreat.

A life forever changed
Once Q Station opened, I became part of the marketing team as Business Development Manager. Then something happened that I never expected. I became pregnant! I was told at the age of twelve that I would never become pregnant - and even if I did by some miracle fall pregnant, my body would never be capable of carrying to full term. *What! Pregnant? No!* I had spent the last twenty years conditioning myself that I did not want to become a mother. After all, I had been told I couldn't, so best to not want it! My new husband had thought long and hard about whether to continue our relationship based on the fact that I couldn't have kids and we had decided that we would just be *really* good travelers and enjoy the disposable income that adults without kids seem to have. The shock turned to excitement and a ton of nerves and eventually ended in a miscarriage. However, by now we knew we could fall pregnant so what else was possible? Aimee... that's what was possible. My beautiful baby girl was placed in my arms at a healthy 4.05kgs. My mum was over the moon and couldn't wait to meet her!

When Aimee turned five months old, I decided to take her to see my mum in the UK for the first time. It was an awful flight as Aimee didn't sleep the whole time and I remember telling my mum that I wouldn't do that again in a hurry. Sadly, during that visit my mum was diagnosed with a life ending illness and I made the difficult decision to relocate and look after her. During that year, I flew from Sydney to London and back four times; each and every flight was terrible as Aimee was unable to sleep during the flight. The airline provides you with a bassinet, but it is directly under a TV, right next to the toilet where people gather the whole flight and subject to the distraction of passers-by, overhead reading lights and cabin lights. It's really difficult to remove these distractions in order to get baby to sleep. I searched for a product to help overcome these difficulties to no avail. It was after my mum passed away and I began to heal that I started to doodle pictures of a product that may overcome this problem - and there my journey into entrepreneurship began!

The birth of the business
I was mourning my mum's death so badly, but there was something about this idea that I couldn't let go of. I had no design or manufacturing experience, but I put a prototype together with plumbers tubing, black out fabric and double sided sticky tape (I can't sew) and I set about designing and developing CoziGo. It's the world's first Multi-Purpose Sleep & Sun Cover for all Strollers, Prams & Airline Bassinets. It's an essential item for getting out and about every day with a baby and a must-have for flying and travel! CoziGo is 100% breathable, blocks 97% of light, can be opened up and used as a sun cover providing UVP of 50+ and is super compact and lightweight. It has fast become known as "The Miracle Cover" for mums that value their babies all-important sleep routine whilst maintaining a healthy outdoor lifestyle.

It took more time, more money and more effort than I ever imagined - but I launched the product to the whole of Australia on the first series of Shark Tank. I gained investment from Janine Allis from Boost Juice and hit the ground running! Mum would have been beside herself with pride!

Mistakes happen
It sounds like a dream run, doesn't it? However, my successes have not come without *many* failures. My biggest hurdle happened before I sold a single unit - my first batch of stock turned up and had to go straight to landfill. That was a $25,000 mistake… I relied on a third party to do quality control and did not fly to China myself! But – in business, it's not the mistakes you make that's important - it's how you fix them. I was very close to giving up that day, but instead I decided to pick myself up, brush myself off, find an alternative manufacturer, place another order and do it properly!

The solopreneur juggle
As a mum of two kids, setting up and running a business and trying to be a good parent was so hard. I learned very quickly that winging it does *not* work. Structure, organisation and routine are critical. At first, I employed an au pair and then realised I had outsourced the most important part of my life. I missed my kids and the guilt was unbearable. I decided that if I couldn't do this alongside being a present, hands on mum – then it would be the business that had to go. So I rearranged life and quite frankly, stopped working as hard. I decided that if it couldn't be done in the time I had –then it would have to wait. I became more structured and strict about everyone's routine. Simple things like writing a to-do list at the end of every day before I log off from work and ensuring that before I go to bed that the kid's lunches are

packed, and their clothes are laid out for the next day. I have to also add here that my beautiful Mother-in-law also offered regular help and agreed to care for Harry for two full days a week! How lucky I felt that my little boy had the pleasure of his Nanna's company whilst I got time to work! My mental and physical health was also suffering – I had a gym membership going unused and I was feeling like crap constantly. So I pledged that I would set the alarm early and get up before everyone else to fit in something for me – meditation, exercise, a cup of tea or just a moment in the garden to reflect! Starting the day the right way is very important for me.

What's next?

Fast forward three years and we are now selling CoziGos all over the world with distribution partnerships in place. I am currently in negotiations with a US distributor and if this pays off, I'm hoping it will be a true match made in heaven (and I'm not going to pretend that the trip to New York that's on the cards, isn't VERY, VERY exciting!). I have so many different product ideas running around in my head. Despite being a risk taker, I've wanted to be very conservative with regard to bringing new products to market. I have wanted to make sure that CoziGo has legs and can provide a positive cash flow in order to expand the brand range. Things are looking really good, so watch this space!

Tips for your entrepreneurial journey

Be brave. Successful entrepreneurs are often not conservative. They take risks. Some of them don't pay off, but they keep trying until one of their ideas pays off!

Budget carefully. Don't risk the family home to follow your dreams. Make sure you have the resources to make your big idea work. Don't forget to leave a budget for marketing as 'build it

and they will come' doesn't work. You need money to tell your customers that you've arrived.
Be organised. Proper planning and preparation go a long way. Routines for the whole family are critical. Until the weekend – and then routines can be chucked out of the window.

Outsource as soon as you can. Stick to what you're good at and outsource the rest as soon as you can afford it. It's a false economy to constantly work in your business at the expense of working *on* your business.

Be kind to yourself. Things will go wrong. Don't beat yourself up if you've made a mistake. Pick yourself up and work out how to fix it as soon as possible so you can leave it behind!

Make time for your partner. When the kids are grown up, you want to be able to turn around and still love the person you made them with! It's important you don't forget how to have fun. My husband are I are both from divorced parents so it's extra important to us to want to stay together. We've been together for twelve years and we still find time for mystery dates. We will invite each other out on a date via text message with no details. As the time gets closer, we may give a dress code or little clues to the evenings or day's event. It's so exciting and romantic. In the past, our mystery dates have been as extravagant as a comedy cruise around the harbour followed by a night in a hotel, to as simple as a secret picnic on a remote beach. One time, Phil filled the back of the car with fire wood and we went to the local dam and had a sausage sizzle!

Jessica McCarroll

First in Breast Dressed

It started with one post. A musing on a blank Facebook page. I reflected back three years to the fourth trimester with my first baby, Lachlan. He sat watching ABC Kids on the other side of the wall. I was 26 weeks pregnant with my second boy, sitting on the bed of a short-term rental. Our house was mid renovation. Hubby was busy renovating it. This was not the support network I had dreamed of surrounding myself with when I vowed to be better prepared as a second-time mum.

My first pregnancy was a dream and I loved every second of it. So much so that when it ended in a less than ideal birthing experience, it hit me harder than a tonne of bricks. Breastfeeding the first night was hard. Lachlan fed constantly for two whole hours. Or at least, so I thought. I had no clue what I was doing, nor did I know the difference between milk transfer and normal comfort sucking. We were both on one hell of a learning journey together. The next day as I continued to try to feed a sleepy baby near constantly, my nipples began to pain. I was no stranger to cracked nipples as a physio; they are something

I had treated before. The midwives told me they looked fine and despite an initial protest, who was I to question them?

Lachlan was perfect in every way to me; however the doctors and child health nurses were quick to point out his lack of weight gain. This is where my breastfeeding troubles began, alongside post-natal depression and anxiety. A vicious cycle ensued until finally eight months postpartum I was able to seek the help I needed for my own mental health. Despite my extensive research and best efforts, Lachlan had weaned from the breast the month before. One thing I had learned during that long struggle was how to breastfeed when things didn't go to plan. I had begun to help friends and online acquaintances in forums with their own breastfeeding struggles and realised that I had information others needed. This is when I started blogging and vowed to become an Internationally Board Certified Lactation Consultant. It was around this time I hit the first stumbling block in my plan... I was jealous of every pregnant and successfully breastfeeding mum I came across. Not a great start to my new career path.

The blogging stopped.

Fast forward two years, seven counsellors, a group therapy program and medication change later, and I was finally ready. I could look at a pregnant woman and not feel the intense fear or anxiety threatening to overwhelm me. I could celebrate a new mum's breastfeeding success without the green eyed monster consuming every inch of me. I was happy for myself and the world around me. One main motto now shaped the forefront of my being: *I am enough.*

I was nervous when we started trying to conceive our second child yet determined to do better. Part of my wellness plan had included a support network; ideally made up of a combination of friends, family, colleagues and acquaintances. I was no stranger to online Mum forums and had always found them to be helpful, and best of all, available! There is *always* someone up when you need them. First in Breast Dressed was born from a desire to feel cushioned by support in an anonymous space. It would be a space I shared knowledge I gained on breastfeeding hints and tips, as well as a space to share my journey. I am Jess from First in Breast Dressed and thankfully, my second time around breastfeeding journey was somewhat better. I decided to lift the veil of anonymity and start a more open conversation with mums interacting with the page.

Mums just like me with the same problems I had faced. Mums I felt empowered to share with and humbled to receive feedback from.

Life with two boys, working part time as a physiotherapist and keeping up with running a small business that's still in its infant stages certainly has its challenges! At this point in time though, I feel it's exactly where I need to be. With so many hours dedicated to breastfeeding and breast health research, it seems a shame not to share and empower others with that knowledge. I am learning to run a business just as I have learned to muddle my way through motherhood. First in Breast Dressed exists within the noisy world of female entrepreneurs targeting a rich Mummy market. This is both exciting and terrifying in the same breath. Akin to motherhood, it brings chances of supportive spaces both online and in person. It also lends to competition from every angle. This is what small business is about and something I feel women bring to a cut throat industry. A sense of collaboration, support and above all, solidarity.

Alongside social media and the blog, I have gathered a collection of products I feel can greatly benefit women on their breastfeeding journey. As a breastfeeding Mum I have put them through the paces and will not stock anything I don't explicitly think is worthy. With a healthcare background, I make it my mission to connect breastfeeding dyads with items that they need.

The biggest rewards I have received out of Mumpreneur life are the new contacts and friends I have found. Genuine women wanting to build women up, rather than tear them down. That is something you don't get in every situation. Solo business can sometimes be lonely, but through the strength of these connections I have been able to be inspired over and over again.

Through the valleys and hills, I would like to shout out to all female entrepreneurs: *You are enough*.

To turn small business into big business, a true passion alongside grit and determination is needed. With that fire and true belief in your cause comes a great ability to succeed in the market. You must also surround yourself with likeminded people, those that believe in you when your belief falters. Support networks structured around building women up instead of tearing each other down. Similarly, you must contribute to this support. You only get out what you put in, and this is true in all facets of life.

The future of First in Breast Dressed holds more time for blogging, working with inspirational women, and a greater focus on breast health as well as breastfeeding. A new line of products is also on the cards. First in Breast Dressed truly aims to support Mumkind, one feed at a time.

Jessica

With kids, they don't do what you want them to do when you want them to do it. Organizations don't necessarily, either. You've got to listen. You've got to learn how to influence.

-Ellen J. Kullman

Karen Koutsodontis

The Travelling Kitchen

I always knew that I would be a mum. Starting my first career as a teacher, I had a love of not only kids, but of building connections and inspiring kids to love to learn. I thought myself to be a pretty good teacher, I was young, enthusiastic, and well-liked by most kids. Perhaps the fact that I taught a pretty fun subject, like food tech, or the old home eco as it was known, meant that kids liked coming to my subject. Little did I know, the impact of having kids of my own on my teaching would have. The shift in my role as a mother made me a better teacher and found me caring more about my students than I thought was possible. I guess becoming a mother not only deepened my love of my own child but deepened the love I have of working with children overall.

So, it came to be that I was really torn after I had my first child (Matteo who is now ten years old). Torn in the fact that I loved being at home with him, loved teaching and the reality of also needing a little income. It would come to be that my school would only let me return if I worked part time, four days a week. Ridiculous, I thought. So, I started wondering how I could continue my love of teaching and working with kids, but work on my own terms. I had a little idea, but not a lot of confidence behind that idea. I thought it wouldn't work, I thought it was too hard, I thought and thought and thought. I knew I had the skills to do what I needed to do, but I thought *what if I fail or what if it can't get if off the ground at all?* It wasn't until my eldest was at kinder that I saw an opportunity to run with my idea and give it a test run.

So, what was my idea exactly? To teach kids - very young kids, kids of all ages, that don't get the chance to learn at school or home - how to cook! There were so many students that I taught in secondary school that came to me knowing very little about food, where it came from, how to cook and what healthy habits looked like. I wondered why we were starting food education so late. Yes, it might be taught sporadically throughout primary school, but why wasn't it more available? Why aren't kids cooking all the time in the younger years? And then I worked out the answer to my question. It was too hard! Often too hard for the classroom teacher to organise the food, equipment, help to run a cooking class themselves, and so forth, and then ka-ching! My idea came to fruition. Take the stress away for the classroom teacher and provide them with that service - a satellite service that would provide a cooking experience at a kindergarten or primary school - and this in part formed the name of my business: The Travelling Kitchen - where our catch phrase is "ZOOMING into a place near you to cook with you!"

So, back to the test run. I trialed the idea at my eldest child's kinder to begin with, and I remember it like it was yesterday. We made homemade jam for Mother's Day. The look on the kids' faces when they saw the fruits of their labour turning strawberries and sugar into jam and packaging it in cute little jars for their mothers, was truly wonderful and inspiring. The kinder teacher thought the idea was a winner and then the idea went on hold again! Baby number two was on the way. My little girl, Milana was born. Being home for number two, I had more time to plan and develop my idea. When she was one and my eldest Matteo started school, I piloted the program through the course of that year with the Prep cohort at his school. Again, it was very well received, and the teachers asked me what I was waiting for, and why I wasn't rolling it out already, and so I did the following year. The start of 2014 Travelling Kitchen made its mark.

I thought I would not be very busy to begin with. I thought it would have taken a while to get known and the phone to start ringing, but it didn't. In the first year of business, we worked with close to 6000 children. I was literally gob smacked and thought I was just incredibly lucky. The next year, we saw close to 8500 kids and again, I was gob smacked and thought it was all about luck. I remember having a conversation with a good friend of mine and talking about the business and how it was going, and how I had been really lucky. She said, "Stop saying that, stop saying you are lucky. It's going well. Start saying that you are proud and that you are working hard to have achieved your success". This was the start of trying to change my mindset around my business. I was starting to get recognised, entering myself for awards, being interviewed on radio, and published in local newspapers about my work. It felt good, but still a little awkward. I have questioned myself a lot in the process of having a business; questioned my beliefs, my desires, and my feelings, and questioned if it's all worth it. But every time I questioned myself, I would always be led back to the answer that the work I do matters, its important, and it changes the lives of kids. That's what fuels me to keep at it.

Along the way, there have been a few bumps. One bump being quite literally a bump with my third child being conceived.

It threw me into meltdown mode for a while as I thought, "My gosh, how am I going to run this business being pregnant, when the baby is born, when I am breastfeeding, when I am having sleepless nights?" It was the best bump I needed as it forced me to take myself out of the front line of the business. I had to hire more staff, I had to delegate, I had to put on a second in charge, and I had to cope with my feelings of having my business run a little less without me. It was hard, and it still is hard as I try to delegate more and more, so I am not wasting time on the day to day running of the business and try to get into more of the 'big picture' stuff. My third baby, little Luca, brought a new level of busyness to our life and a new level of stress to the business, as I needed it to make enough to pay my ever-growing staff and leave me a little on top of that, and thankfully, it has managed to do that. We keep increasing our turnover year after year, and each year I have been able to step a little further away from this baby, The Travelling Kitchen.

When I think back to the days before Travelling Kitchen, so much has changed. I have changed as a person, having learnt so much, my mind extending way beyond what I thought it could. From book keeping, social media management, HR, budgeting, goal setting, team building, managing staff, there are so many new skills I have acquired. I am way busier than I have ever been, but I love the work I do, and I love that it makes a difference, and my kids see that I am doing something I love doing. I couldn't have done it without the help of my extended family and their support with the care of my children, the childcare they go to and also a little home help with a cleaner. A food swap with a bunch of mums to stock our freezer with meals has also been a life saver. A little while ago, I was chatting to my eldest and I asked him, "What do you think of mummy selling The Travelling Kitchen and just being a stay at home mum - would you like that?" And he said, "No mummy, you can't do that, your work is too important for kids and you love it". I knew then that I was setting a perfect example for him and my other two kids, too.

When I look to the future now for Travelling Kitchen, I no longer think *what if, what if I fail, what if I can't do it?* I think, look at how much I have achieved in a few short years and there is still so much to do. I am not nervous about the future as much as I used to be, I am excited. We plan to increase the number of kids we visit each year, giving them great food memories. We also plan to launch a national campaign, franchise and extend our work into other states and publish a book about the wonders of cooking.

For other mums who have read my story and wonder, *Could I? Should I? What if?* I hope you take all those doubts and nerves in reading a story like this and transform them into feelings that inspire action and creativity to drive your idea out of your head and into action. Don't doubt yourself, trust yourself. Don't waste time, make use of the time. If your gut says it's a good idea, then it usually is. If your kids are little, enlist as much support as you can get and freely accept it, without feeling guilty. And, expect that there will be storms along the way, but you are strong enough to get through them. Learn through them and grow through them. You are more than a mum. You are amazing, and you can do anything. We tell our kids this and want them to believe it, so we should too!

Karen

Katharine Rattray

Kat & Fox

Once upon a time there was a blonde little girl with big blue eyes who dreamed, and dreamed big. One day she was going to change the world and make a million dollars. That was little me, Kat, and now I am a typical forty-something woman striving to find her truth. Writing this has been sparked by recent events where my life back flipped and spun out of control.

Who am I? Katharine Rattray, a mother to three crazies and small business owner who has been described in many words: enthusiastic, creative, bubbly, chatty, loud, blunt, impulsive, funny, a friend, a mother, posh, English eccentric, crazy, a wife, a daughter, an artist, an actress, a teacher, bossy, friendly, loving and unique.

Sorry for the clichés - *and there will be many throughout this* - but I would say that I am a square peg who endeavoured for so long and so hard to squeeze into the round hole of her life. Here I write *my* tale of how the tunes of others that I chose to groove along to, took me on a journey/a path of life, where I soared to the highest of highs and then nose-dived into the depth of despair.

I grew up as Katharine Jane Fox, a true-blue Brit. Yes, I'm a very proper pommy from Surrey on the outskirts of London, with a big old plum in her mouth! Growing up, I was surrounded by super high achievers. In my world, if you didn't have buckets of money, good breeding and had completed a university course, you were lower class and an 'insignificant' human. This was drilled into my little blonde head, and my blue eyes saw a future measuring the ability to succeed and be accepted by financial and academic achievement. My parents' expectations were to follow in the footsteps of past members of the Fox clan and head towards a rather 'beige' career in accountancy or medicine. The difficulty was that I was more 'orange' than 'beige' with a splash of 'magenta'. I always felt as if I was different. Could this have been because I had suffered a severe seizure when I was three years old, with a two-year stint on the drug Phenobarbitone, resulting in regular hospital visits for brain scans resulting in a life long struggle with my mental health? Or perhaps, was I an alien from another planet? *The latter, me thinks.*

Seriously, I have no idea, but my parents desperately tried to sculpt their little blonde darling to fit the expectation of the Fox clan. It was like trying to contain a screeching feline in a small tin box; loud and scary. The vibrant colours within me revealed themselves in a variety of different ways: dramatic and overly emotive, fidgety, and a relentless scribbler who would conjure up characters from stories and spend time disappearing into the back garden to make new, colourful worlds. The words 'behave' and 'focus' were regularly flung at me from teachers. However, they politely ignored this 'difference' and encouraged me to follow in the footsteps of my brother who was on the well mapped out path of academia into the world of medicine.

How did the 'tunes' of other's help me to define success?

Due to all this bullshit, I understood that success was measured with a checklist of oversized tick boxes, which I had compiled by listening to the direction of others. I etched this into my soul and subsequently, my twenties and thirties were all about achieving as much as I could and damn well ticking those boxes with full velocity. I truly felt this would inevitably assist me in climbing the rickety ladder of life - transitioning me to the final expected level of ultimate mind-blowing success. Finally, I would gain the all imperative approval I desired. I really believed that without my parents/others' approval, I was nothing.

You probably believe by now that all of this went swimmingly, and I am in fact writing this while lazing on a six-foot yacht in the middle of the Maldives, dripping with abundant diamonds, exhibiting an ironed out face full of cow fat, sunning myself, and having my feet massaged by a chunk of hunk tanned god called Hans.

Sadly, the truth and to no real surprise, no. The formula I had imprinted into me as a child should have worked by my mid-forties. HUGE reality check. No, no and again can I say fucking no… ARGHHHHH!

Ticking the boxes…probably not the best plan.

I set out in my teens with my success checklist in hand:

- Go to university
- Travel the world

- Get a great job and earn good money
- Meet the man of my dreams
- Get married
- Buy a house
- Get a dog
- Have a baby or ten
- Get a bigger house
- Add in a few promotions
- Add in lots of holidays to make your friends green with envy
- Buy a bigger house with a pool
- Retire
- Buy a Winnebago and travel Australia as a grey nomad
- Die

Sound familiar?

Let's start with uni. Off I bounded to complete my Fine Arts degree, paintbrush and endless enthusiasm in hand. Year One was fantastic as I spent the year painting breasts, wrapping myself in wire, and creating sculptures that were exploring my ongoing atypical detest for my physical form. Yes, I absorbed a lot of Silvia Plath that year and took on my feministic approach to life in general. The second year bought me a scholarship to an art school in Nice, France. The experience was gold, but my brain took charge and I fell into a heap not understanding what was wrong with me. This resulted in a diagnosis of clinical depression and my inability to complete the course. I was left broken. I sat there for months staring into space whilst slumped on the sofa in the confines of my parents' front lounge. Disillusionment in everything was further cultivated. I doubted my initial choice of studying Fine Art and swore I didn't want to end up as *just* an art teacher like my fellow class mates were destined for. Oh my God, a failed attempt at uni. No tick in that box. It was a hard road to recovery, but after two years living with my parents and working in good old retail selling for a well-known American clothing chain, whilst polishing my American plastic personality, I decided enough was enough. The pull was there... and I just had to... I needed to succeed. I started to listen to MY tunes. Me being me, I threw together a damned fine folio as I decided a career in interior design was for me. A career where I could spend the days sewing curtains and arranging cushions. *'A pillow fluffer'... that's what it was all about...... wasn't it?"*

I was accepted into the Interior Architecture Degree at Brighton University. *That's the same as interior design,* was my thought process, *I am sure it is. I'll be fine.* Wrong, *big* wrong. The first year was cool: drawing, playing and experimenting in more ways than one. It flowed beautifully. I smashed all the projects thrown my way. I was the top student for year one of the course. Second year was a different story. I forgot to mention that yes, I was excellent at art, but when it came to anything numbers-based I was like a confused frog with four thumbs and a peace pipe...what a disaster zone! Structural engineering and materials was the name of the game in the second year. Oh boy, did I struggle! I was determined to tick the uni box, so I persisted with all the night sessions and tutoring. It didn't work and half way through that second year, I experienced my second bout of fucking depression and burn out. *No way, again! What the hell is wrong with me? Do you see the familiar thread running through my journey? Why can't I just tick that bloomin' uni box?*

The next best thing for me was to secure a job, work my arse off and tick the 'travel the world' box. This would be a chance to clear my head and work out how I could return to the UK and finally achieve that oh-so desired degree.

Going well are we?

Well, you'd think this would be smooth sailing? Yes, three boxes were ticked within a six-month time frame during my travels! I know, I know, yay for me, but how? Being the young buxom blonde I was, I met a fine, young specimen of an Aussie boy, fell in lust with his accent and was shockingly up the duff within three weeks of us commencing the union. My life flipped again, and I became his defacto and an Australian resident. WTF? *Are you seeing the pattern here?*

Time to update the boxes ticked:

- I have the man
- Birthed the ten-pound baby critter
- Travelled part of the globe alone

Perfect. Three of my boxes ticked.

Now, for uni. *Could I do it?* To be honest, we were in our mid-twenties and all we possessed was a backpack of grubby hippie clothes and a rather dilapidated Kombi van with blue waves and bubbles painted on the side. Adding to this picture, a soft, round bundle of spew, poo and high-pitched shrieks. Not looking good, me thinks. That's okay - there will always be another time. I'll just make it work in Australia. I may have to alter the tick boxes slightly. I'm sure I can do that. I wasn't sure of all the rules and regulations when it came to the 'tick box to success' approach.

I was really becoming accustomed to this roller coaster called 'Kath's life'. So, I set myself a mantra: *"I'll be a great wife, find some kind of employment and be the best mother a child could ask for. Think about it, it's all a new beginning!"* I stared into the mirror and through the relentless burning tears, I repeated this daily until it became a reality.

For ten years, I managed to jam myself into that round hole and hide the pain as it built up and up to an intoxicating level. I look back and I can't believe that for a decade, my life was all about fitting in. I was being 'normal'.

So, let's tick some more boxes...

- Bought a house
- Then another
- Had two more beautiful little humans to boot
- Managed to carve a career in the art and design industry through running my own small interior design business and working as a teacher

Yes, a bloody art and design teacher at the local TAFE. I obtained two diplomas in education and interior design. Life was going well. I was ticking even more boxes and people respected me. *Me*, I had respect. Maybe I have a brain. OMG maybe I am worthy. I felt I had it all. I had my cake and ate it.

Failing was shit, but the best thing ever.

To others, my life was perfect; happily married, beautiful home, three happy children and a designer dog called Sadie. Adding to this, I had worked up the ladder in my teaching job earning good dollars. My dear husband had worked hard to build his own business. It was all 'coming up roses', as the saying goes. Why was it that slowly, gradually my capabilities started to decline? The pain turned from a subtle niggle to a full-blown crippling choking, burning sensation. I was in a state of overwhelm and confusion and something had to change and change it did. My father passed away and I birthed an unplanned third child, a baby girl. Straight after she was born, I felt this insane urge that I was going to be an entrepreneur. *I mean, that's what you do, isn't it?* I threw myself onto the 'Mumpreneur' train. Here, I started to tune out from others and find my own beat, the one from deep inside. I took *my* passion for children's illustration from a hobby into a money-making venture. First, it was personalized Name Arts, then greeting cards which were sold through market stalls. I had my baby strapped on my front in the ergo pouch, and my two little boys by my side. I remember it was very fast, impulsive and exciting. I worked tirelessly and built my first attempt at a brand, 'Doodlebugs'.

Business was good, and orders were flying in left, right and centre. But with no planning – just creating – it all grew too big, too fast and I ended up collapsing in my local shopping centre with an irregular heart beat and burn out.

Let me tell you, it was an amazing ride at the time, but the mess left behind wasn't too enthralling. For the following eight months, I could not pick up a pencil and draw, my hand would physically shake, my creativity had killed me. I resented it and felt hollow. The only solution was to refocus and get back to the place I was before – 'the Katharine that fit's in' – journeying back to the safe, high paid job and working on growing *our* possessions and enjoying our holidays. 'Keeping up with the Jones.' Nightly, I stared at my reflection in the mirror and told myself, *This is what you are. This is your life. Do not deviate EVER again*. My own tune had faded to a distant mumble. My self-worth was shot, and I allowed every 'negatron' comment from others to absorb into me. The stress built up again, mistakes were made, and others became upset with me. My brain fogged over, and I felt as if I was living a shell-like existence. I was so distressed in my teaching job. I was the feline in the tin box... *remember her?* As in all educational environments, I loved what I did, but the expectations were high and I was exhausted, stressed, embarrassed and alone. I really felt trapped and the only way out was to jump ship.

TIME OUT. I returned to the UK to reconnect with my family in 2015. By going back to my roots, I had the opportunity to clearly see my truth flash before my eyes and the mumble turned back into the music I needed to hear from deep within. This came in the guise of Kat & Fox, a name I chose for my new venture to honour my late father and a nod to the young girl with the pure heart from all those years ago. My heart was bursting as the passion returned. The colour came back to my cheeks - the orange and magenta that made me so 'different' glimmered in its brilliance. I spent hours designing, drawing and creating. I developed a business plan. A children's book and a collection of children's linen was birthed into the world in super vibrant hues. I was on fire. I saw the big - the massive - and I was ravenous for recognition and success. Others were amazed and supportive as not only was I building my brand three days a week, but I was also back teaching two days a week for financial reasons. *You know, mortgage, kids and all that goes with motherdom.* Everything was looking peachy. I was putting myself and the brand out there through social media platforms, networking, tradeshows and gaining recognition by winning awards. I was on the highest of highs. My inner fire was constantly fueled and fed by the words of others, but my ears were deaf to the ones that mattered the most. My friends and family.

I disappeared for hours on end into my studio, took ridiculous risks and spent a lot of money without thinking, resigning to the fact that this was what I had to do to make it BIG and make it big quick. Shit, I was in a hurry.

The snowball grew, and it grew fast, and I was lost inside. I detached from my children and my husband. I could not understand why they would not support me anymore and I began to see them as the enemy, the naysayers. I arrived at a point where I believed in the brand so much, I organised a contract for a ridiculous amount of stock to be manufactured. At the advice of my Australian based agent, I signed this believing it was a brave leap forward and a positive move. This was where the next low point began – both the best and worst thing that could have happened to me. I could not sell the volumes of stock and meet the payments; the strain was huge, and everything felt out of control. The tune I was hearing now was like a funeral march and 'Kat & Fox' was becoming a thorn in my side.

But I had created Kat, my professional name, and she kept a smilin' and a wavin' so no one knew. My husband's anger and negativity grew to the point of verbal abuse… he could not understand and was afraid. He saw what we had built together falling into ruins. Hurtful words like rocks were hurled at me from the ones I thought loved and supported me. The cracks were starting to reveal themselves; the façade I had created was tumbling. Sales declined, pneumonia set in, which caused the worst bout of depression, and I was left lying in a hospital bed in a state of despair. Yes, I had built a popular brand and that was great, but it was also a consuming monster that was gobbling me up. My eyes grew heavier with every step forward. A fog gathered in my head, making every day a struggle. Looking back, it was devastating to think that my babies witnessed me fall to floor wailing - desperate to end it all. Again, the feline trapped in the tin box with the lid firmly stuck shut. *Why was I like this?* I listened to the wrong and loudest tunes. I was deaf to the beautiful one within me and the ones of those who mattered and cared the most - my dear friends and family.

It wasn't over yet...

The final straw was the day I won the prestigious AusMumpreneur award for Network Excellence. At the same moment I won the award, I received text from my husband to say that he had left me. From joy to despair in one fleeting moment. I had hit the murky bottom of the deep, dark well, or so I thought... more was to come in the form of a diagnosis of Bipolar Type 2. This was a huge label for me to digest. I was incapacitated for two months whilst coming to terms with it all, trialing drugs and working through how I was to travel forward. I had well and truly been stripped of it all. It was confronting to name and pigeon hole my behaviours but finding out about the condition was the saving grace I needed. It all started to make sense - the up and downs, successes and failures, disconnections and connections. Now, the fog is starting to lift and I have begun to work on rebuilding myself by building a tribe around me of good friends, family, medical and business professionals. I know it will never be easy, but hey, when is life ever easy? Gradually, I can feel vibrancy in my life again. I am returning to the studio, connecting with my children, and learning to quiet my busy mind. I am so sappy that I am finally dancing to the beat of my own tunes, stating daily:

That's a great idea Kat, but let it go for today... one thing at a time lady cakes, and hey, are you okay? Have a cup a tea and take ten.
Yes, I have learnt a LOT...

And finally...

Once I was an innocent, fresh faced and wide-eyed teen. Now I feel as if the innocence has been revisited and been draped with the gift of wisdom. Now and only now, through repetitive mistakes and impulsive acts, I can honestly say this:

When you are living according to others' expectations and you put your own life to the side, life takes deviations and you end up dragging yourself through it, trying to fit in with others. This leads to a life of turmoil and one never realises what is actually happening. Did I always have a mental health condition, or did it eventuate through undue repeated stressors? I have no idea. By arriving at the place I am now, I can honestly say that I am okay, that I went through all of this for me to be the woman I am today. Who is she? One who stands tall in her own truth, dancing to her own tune.

Now, it's time for me to slow the pace and make smaller, more realistic goals to chip away at. It is time to take delight in who I am today, with the love that surrounds me from the children I birthed, and the friends that were there to catch me when I fell. The past failures have taught me about pacing myself. I also now have what I need to be truly passionate about the gift of creativity that I have been blessed with, and the colour I can bring to the world through the artworks I create. I can also celebrate the smiles on faces I bring through my zest for life and laughter. I love the entrepreneurial journey I started, and Kat & Fox is not lost; it will and is evolving into something that fits with MY life, MY truth, MY tune.

I work really hard at trying to see the big picture and not getting stuck in ego. I believe we're all put on this planet for a purpose, and we all have a different purpose... When you connect with that love and that compassion, that's when everything unfolds.

-Ellen DeGeneres

Melissa Woodward

Evolution Health Services

Becoming a Mum and a business owner within a six-month period was not something I had originally planned. But it has been the greatest decision and biggest challenge of my life. Evolution Health Services was started four years ago after the birth of my son, Blake. Alongside my husband, Tristan, we decided to start a business focused on health and fitness for families.

I have always had a passion for helping women through pregnancy and into motherhood. It started when I saw the struggles my Mum and Sister went through with their bodies following pregnancy. In the past I let my fears of not being a Mum stop me from working with Mums. Tristan wanted to help Dads to have the fitness to be able to play with their kids and to help kids get fit while having fun. Together we felt it was a great combination for helping the whole family.

It took me a long time to really discover myself, find my confidence and ask for what I wanted in life.

I have been a Remedial Massage Therapist for fifteen years and a Personal Trainer for five years. When studying to become a Massage Therapist, it seemed easy as I was straight out of High School. I was still in the swing of studying and didn't have to work full time. However, it took me ten years and three courses to finally become a qualified Personal Trainer.

I first started my fitness qualifications in 2003. I was working full time, so studying was at night, after work. After finishing my Gym Instructor qualification, my personal life was less than happy. I had ended a relationship with a guy I lived with. I found myself living back with my family and couldn't bring myself to attend TAFE. I gave up the course and focused on repairing my personal life.

In 2005 I tried again. I started working for Fitness First. As I was already qualified as a Gym Instructor, it allowed me to work as a Personal Trainer under supervision for a year while I studied. I was working long hours, 6 days per week. I opened the gym at 5:45am, sometimes seeing clients until 8 or 9pm. I had also started my own massage business from home. It was a competitive environment at the gym and at home I was hiding from the world as I lacked confidence in running my own business. I felt everyone else was better than me and I needed to learn more. I tried focusing on study in the middle of the day but often I just needed a nap.

As I approached the end of the first year, I had 2 subjects to go before completion. But again, my next relationship fell apart. It was a very traumatic relationship and decisions made during our time together resulted in long term consequences. I had lost all confidence in myself and my abilities. I needed security and stability. I chose to leave my passion and find a full-time job as a Case Manager in Workers Compensation.

Over the years, I had moments of wanting to return and moments where I had given up any hope of returning. At one point I threw out my books, notes, videos, everything except my massage table. I tried selling my table once, but it ended up travelling around with me wherever I went. Just prior to this time, I thought about starting to massage again. I was in another relationship where it was all about helping him follow his dreams and mine were not considered. There was a pattern here. Whenever I was in a relationship I focused on helping them and never valued my dreams enough. It wasn't their fault, it was mine. For giving up when things got tough, not asking for what I wanted and not having the confidence to push past the self-doubt.

Once I put myself in a position where I was independent and happy on my own, I met Tristan at work. We developed a friendship at first and realised we really clicked. Early into our relationship we discovered we both wanted the same things in life and had been through some very similar situations. We had a shared passion for the health and fitness industry. He had also attempted his fitness qualifications but didn't quite make it to becoming a qualified Personal Trainer.

We decided to complete our personal training course together while working full time. It was so wonderful to find someone who had the same passion and a relationship where we supported each other to achieve more. It was tough keeping motivated and juggling work, but we pushed each other. It almost became a little competitive with who had submitted the most assessments.

Early in the course, I lost my Aunty who was very close to me. This time I didn't give up. I may have had a few tantrums and procrastinated more than I would like to admit but I kept going. I pushed past my desire to give up. Later in the course, I found out that I was pregnant. I was suffering morning sickness from about seven weeks, but instead of giving up, I felt this deadline to get it finished.

At fifteen weeks pregnant we finished the course. After so many attempts, we finally did it!

Becoming a Mum seemed to be the real driver for me to finish. It was no longer about me alone. I had a baby on the way who needed someone who was ready to push through the tough times and not give up. This has continued throughout our business as we are constantly faced with tough times. When you have a family to support, there is a new level of drive that keeps you pushing. Pushing you past the fears, past the desire to give up, to become the role model for our son. He is the inspiration for our business and the reason we strive to continue our success.

I was now a Mum. I was on maternity leave from my Worker's Compensation role. I struggled with the idea of returning to work so far from home. I had been watching the Mums I worked with arriving early in the morning before everyone else. I would see them have to leave at 4:30pm to make the commute back to daycare before it closed at 6pm. They missed out on seeing their kids for twelve hours every day, only to make it home in time for dinner, baths and bed.

I heard negative comments made about their working arrangements. How they were off again because of their sick kids. Or comments about their ability in their role on part time hours. At the time, I didn't completely comprehend all that was happening, but I guess it was all sinking into the back of my mind. As I contemplated my own return to work, I could see that by returning to work in that environment, I would be missing so much. I may have negative comments said about me and maybe I wouldn't be valued in my role unless I chose to return to full time hours.

Maternity leave was my ticket out of there, but I couldn't yet see what I was able to do outside of the insurance industry. I wanted to work again as a Massage Therapist but wasn't sure where to start. There were not many jobs as a Massage Therapist or Personal Trainer that didn't involve rent or working as sub-contractor. I had to think about all the skills and experiences I had gained over the years. I had been in business in the past, I had experience in the health and fitness industry and had plenty of qualifications I could utilise. However, having failed in my business in the past and having struggled with self-doubt and confidence, I was nervous about making the move. However, I found the confidence to get started with Tristan's support and Blake as my inspiration.

Our business had very small beginnings. I originally set up our garage with a space to see massage clients. I started working with a local Osteopath to get back into the industry, while Tristan continued to work full time in Workers Compensation. He soon decided he was sick of missing out on seeing Blake. He wanted to quit his job and start Outdoor Group Training. When Tristan left work, he cashed in his company shares and annual leave. This was what we would live off, as well as use to start the business. It wasn't a huge amount of money, but we were confident.

We bumbled around for a while without a solid plan. In less than six months, the business hadn't taken off enough to support us. The money had dried up and Tristan had to go back to work. It was a tough time as Tristan struggled to find a job heading up to Christmas. It was also coming up to Blake's first birthday. We didn't think we would be celebrating that milestone as we were broke. I felt terrible that we were heading towards failure and wouldn't have any money for a small party or presents. When I cried Tristan would try reassuring me Blake wouldn't know any different, but I would.

Tristan took on any work he could find. He worked unloading containers, driving trucks and got us through. I continued to work as much as I could, around caring for Blake. In the New Year, he secured a full-time job, but it paid significantly less than he was previously earning in Workers Compensation. This meant I really had to keep the business going to make up the difference.

Tristan had been helping take care of our son and nephew, so I could work more massage hours and study. Going back to work meant I needed to take back that responsibility, as well as massage hours, studying and fitness classes.

After a couple of months of juggling our new roles, the juggle got too much. Instead of letting our business fail, we went all in.

With no savings in the bank and Tristan in a lower paying full-time job, I left my massage job to start working from home. I started by seeing massage clients on days my sister could look after Blake and after Tristan would get home from work. I also began running morning classes for mums wanting to get fit. As I had always wanted to work with mums I felt I now had the experience that could effectively help them with their health. I understood the sleep deprivation, the changes that happen to your body, how hard it can be to recover from pregnancy and the lack of knowledge around it all.

Working from home didn't last long. After three weeks of working at home, I got sick of cleaning up the house after a walking one-year old trashed it again. I also remembered the limitations in place by working at home. I was hiding, partly because I didn't want to be seen to be stealing clients from my previous workplace, as well as for the safety of my son. I needed to get out there and I needed to get found. If I wanted to be serious about creating a job for myself and my husband, I needed to take a giant leap.

I started the process of getting found by putting myself out there and connecting with other local small business owners. It began when I found a local ladies networking group called Linking Ladies. I had made the decision to work from home but had not yet created a plan or vision of our business. My shy nature had me sitting by myself and surveying the group. I had to push myself to get up and talk to a familiar face. My attempt bombed, and I sat back down. I had no idea what to say to these women as I had no idea what I was doing.

Each month I attend Linking Ladies, my confidence grew, as well as my connections. I thought networking was all about gaining clients. But it has become a goldmine of knowledge, support, friendships and an understanding for what I am going through as a mum trying to create a business. In time, I found clients through networking, but the most important was the people that I now know to help build my business. I started to create a vision and plan which our business previously lacked.

The ladies got to witness the growth of my business and I'm still in contact with many of these ladies three years later. A few of these women are key advisors or supports in my business today. In 2015, I was awarded 'Start Up Business of The Year' by my fellow Members. I was shocked to win the award but felt so grateful to be appreciated for the work I had put into growing our business.

I continue to network on a weekly basis for my business and for my own personal development. I am a member of the local Chamber of Commerce and support our local Start Up Mum chapter. These groups have given me the chance to network with males and females, as well as present my business, share my passion and even share my advice on growing a small business. I have gained the confidence to speak to a room full of business owners and know that I have something valuable to offer with my experience. It's a big change from the girl who could barely strike up a conversation.

I have received support, advice and encouragement from people who have been running businesses for as long as thirty years. It's amazing to know that there are so many people out there willing to help you succeed in business. I have found opportunities to collaborate, opportunities to sponsor events and to market through player sponsorship at our local AFL Club. Recently I was encouraged to stand for the position of President of the Campbelltown chapter of the South West Networking Group. This opportunity helped me to grow my skills in leadership and support other local business owners to understand the value of networking.

So, six weeks after starting my massage clinic at home, I found a Physiotherapy clinic looking to lease a room. I got up the courage to ask the question about cost. I also discovered another Massage Therapist and High School friend was looking to leave her home clinic to get out there. We both needed the room on different days, so it worked perfectly. We could share the cost of the rent and support each other in building our businesses.

My way of business budgeting became about 'How many massages do I need to do to pay for this?' It was how I made the decision to take on a commercial lease and how I set my client targets each week. We received a small loan from both of my parents to assist with the upfront costs. I also invested money into learning more about digital marketing to help with my goal of getting found and growing our business.

I had found a passionate mum, who was the guest speaker at my first Linking Ladies Meeting. Serena Ryan was the owner of Serena Dot Ryan. She shared her knowledge about digital marketing and I felt it was exactly what I needed to get found. Initially we spent a whole day in a workshop, creating the template for my website, learning how it all worked and making sure we had the correct keywords in place.

I spent more time learning about social media, email marketing and blog writing. I spent hours and hours creating website content, writing blogs, creating newsletters and posting on social media. Once I understood the process, I created a way to make it my own and deliver it in a way that worked for me. I often get asked if I have a written, structured social media plan, but the secret is that I often complete everything ad hoc. I write as I'm inspired, I share events I'm attending, I even share my massage availability to help potential clients see we have time to help them.

After one week of our website going live, I was ranking on page one in the Google search for 'Remedial Massage Campbelltown'. Currently, we sit in first position on the first page of Google and around 80% of my new clients come from Google searches. It has remained in this position due to my commitment to update my blogs containing the keywords and creating content that I can share on Facebook and in our email newsletter. Blog writing has given me the opportunity to share my stories, my advice about massage, fitness, health and family life. I have achieved my goal to be found and for my business to grow.

Our business growth has not come without it's challenges. While my client base was growing in the new clinic space, my fellow Massage Therapist's business was not. She was a mum of two boys. She had a limited family support network around her and her husband worked full time. She was trying to move clients from her home clinic that were used to paying lower massage fees as well as changing the hours she worked in a clinic setting. They were reluctant to pay more for the same service she was providing at home, and she appeared to lack confidence in charging what she was worth.

Through this time, Tristan and I were also planning our wedding. I don't know what we were thinking and sometimes I wonder how we got through it all. Four weeks before the wedding, she gave notice that she wouldn't be able to rent the room any longer. We had an agreement that she would stay for twelve months but I decided to let it go. Mostly because I had confidence that my business would continue to grow to cover the rent, but also because

I didn't want to make it any more difficult for her family life. After our wedding, we decided to put Blake in daycare two days per week alongside my nephew, so I could take on another day in the clinic to earn enough to cover the rent.

I was lucky enough to have family support around me. From day one of returning to work, my sister and I had been juggling care of my son and nephew to help each other out. My family has been our biggest support network. They were our first clients, share everything we are promoting on Facebook, refer their friends and are always willing to help with babysitting.

Our next challenge came when Tristan was ready to join me again in the business on a full-time basis. One week after finishing up his full-time job, Tristan suffered an injury to his knee while training to be an MMA Fighter. Yes, we are very supportive of each other's dreams, however crazy they sound. We were left in a position where we only had one income to support our family and it was mine from the business.

Tristan tried to continue as many classes as he could, but a Personal Trainer needs to have a certain level of fitness to work. Luckily, most of our clients had been with us for a while, so he could cue them verbally without demonstrating. We had a backup plan with my sister studying fitness to become a Trainer. But one night at training she rolled her ankle and we spent the next few hours in the hospital emergency department. They both had a long recovery ahead of them. I remember feeling alone and the weight of it all on me. My husband was heading for surgery and my back up plan was gone.

We juggled our fitness timetable through his injury as much as possible. When it came time to go in for surgery, I kept up my massage bookings, ran most of our classes, covered his Personal Training clients and attended networking events to keep the momentum going for our business. It became about prioritising my time and ensuring I balanced work with rest.

We called on our connections for help. We arranged with our local PCYC gym for our clients to attend the classes on nights I couldn't run. In return we would cover the costs of their attendance. It allowed our clients to continue with minimal disruption due to our circumstances.

One thing I was passionate about creating was a supportive nature with other business owners. This included those that many would consider my competition.

There was enough work out there for everyone, we all had our different strengths and experiences, so I decided if we worked together we could create a more professional image for massage, fitness and small business. Working with the PCYC really proved that it was possible to help support another business who is considered your competition. Tristan currently works with the PCYC as president of their fundraising committee to give back to the club and the local community.

While having Tristan out of action, it was a proud moment for me. That moment when I realised that my work had generated enough income to support my family while he recovered from surgery. I never missed a month of rent, we paid every bill and because we are completely crazy, we decided to take another giant leap. We took the steps to move and grow our clinic again.

I was outgrowing my clinic room and we had been working towards finding an indoor space for our fitness business. The vision was originally to find a space that would also allow us to build massage rooms to have another massage therapist work alongside myself. We were so close to finding a property, we even made an offer to purchase an industrial unit to suit our business. We missed out when another matching offer was made on the property and they paid their deposit first. We shelved that idea when we were unable to find anything suitable.

We realised most of our income was coming from massage. It didn't quite suit being an addition to a fitness space; it deserved its own suitable location. We found a large, quiet space alongside other health professionals. The only catch was it was a completely open space. No walls, no offices, and it was much larger than we needed. The rent for the section of the space we needed was equivalent to what I was already paying in rent. So I thought of another business who was in need of their own space.

Serena Dot Ryan, the business, needed a permanent home. I approached Serena about looking at the space and after considering the terms, agreed to come on board. We recruited Tristan to build the walls to create our new space. He was almost recovered and had experience in building to save us the cost of hiring a builder. We faced more challenges with trying to gain council approval, the hours of work involved in building and the juggle to keep building walls outside of business hours so that we could continue to see clients.

In a way, it was beneficial that Tristan hadn't had a chance to build his Personal Training client base, so he had the time to put into building. It was a long process of frames, plastering and painting. After two months, we finally had completed walls for all four of our rooms and had created a large waiting room and reception area. Serena also had a training room, office and recording studio created in her space. We have continued to work on the space over the past year, making it better. We finally let Tristan return to his fitness classes, personal training clients and building the client base we had hoped to have for our business.

Today, Evolution Health Services operates the whole clinic space without Serena. She relocated her business and we are focused on continuing to grow. We currently employ two casual Remedial Massage Therapists who can work close to home and have flexible working arrangements to suit their family life.

Personally, I am following my passion for helping mums throughout their pregnancy and post-natal recovery. After suffering a miscarriage with my first pregnancy, my experiences in pregnancy and the recovery from a caesarean section, I have been able to connect with mums through sharing my stories. I am at a point where I truly believe in myself, my knowledge and know that I am enough. While I continue to learn, I am spending more time doing as I have the confidence to put myself out there.

While we still have a vision for a dedicated fitness space, that is a project we quietly work on in the background. When the time is right, we will take the next giant leap.

As we are now in a stable position in the business, we are seeing the growth in turnover too. We have a much more sophisticated accounting method than the 'how many massages' method. Each quarter our accountant shares the figures of how much we have grown. This last quarter we have turned over twice as much in three months than we did in our whole first year.

I never imagined that we could generate these figures from a massage and fitness business.

Looking back, I could have let the fears and failures cripple me, but instead I use them to drive me to move forward. We found ways to overcome obstacles and a new perspective on reaching our goals. Our future is looking positive. We have identified our potential areas of growth.

We continue to juggle our schedules to make sure Blake gets plenty of time at home with us. I get to spend every Monday at home with him and my nephew. The boys both love coming to training, but we are aware that Blake needs early nights and a somewhat normal routine. Our life is hectic, but we appreciate being able to have the flexibility to be there for him if he is sick or has a special event on at school.

If you have read my story and thought that getting into business is too hard, I would encourage you to see the strength and power you can discover in yourself. It has not been easy, but the benefits sure outweigh the negatives in my situation. I could have settled for a stable job but would have traded hours missed with my son and no job satisfaction for that income.

If you are looking to get started, I encourage you to look at the skills you have gained in your years in the workforce prior to becoming a mum. Find what you are passionate about and how you can help others in the process. How can you use those skills and passion to create a job for yourself and where could it lead? I remember being told, "If you can imagine it, you can have it". I could never have imagined this at the beginning, but our vision has evolved over time as we could see what was possible.

The advice I would like to leave you with most is to never give up. While your path may not be straight, know there is another way around obstacles. There is always a way to achieve your dream.

Believe in yourself, believe in what you do and know others will believe in you too. Believe you are enough.

Karen McDermott

Serenity Press / Making Magic Happen Academy

My story is not a conventional life story. In fact, it is not a life story really, it's a story of the past ten years of my life. I don't do things by halves, but I do pursue everything I desire with loving intention which has led to me becoming a serial entrepreneur even though I am also a hands-on mum of six children age ranging from 3 to 22. They are my life, my heart beams when I think of these little (and big) humans I created. They are my life, and my heart beams when I think of these little (and big) humans I created.

I am originally from Ireland, however I moved to Australia in 2008, with my husband and two boys for an adventure of a lifetime. I arrived in Perth thirty-five weeks pregnant with my first daughter, armed with an unwavering knowing that what we were doing was the best thing ever for us. It was totally against all rational thinking, but I have since discovered that most 'knowing' scenarios are often initially perceived as unconventional and it takes courage to pursue what you are being drawn to. We had just finished building a brand-new house in Ireland, a few months before that we got married and I had two boys aged twelve and two to think about, but the call was fierce, and I was ready for some magic. The previous two years had been very dark which took me a while to process as I was so used to the light.

My knowing was very strong. I knew that I was exactly where I was supposed to be, even though being away from my family was really tough. I was the eldest of six and saw my family every single day. I kept my mind busy and away from the fact I was on the other side of the world, so when I felt an urge to write children's books for my son to educate him about Australia, I ran with it. My heart sang, and I would sit and illustrate them for hours around our kitchen table and at night when the kids would go to bed. The process of creating these books was very soul nourishing. I would make them into little books, putting them together in a program I found online and printing them off on a printer I convinced my hubby I needed. My twelve-year-old son said that I should call myself Mamma Mac, which I loved, so I designed my own logo and said that they were home-made children's books. I felt a knowing to contact Princess Margaret Children's Hospital because if I was going to make something of these, then the humanitarian in me wanted some good to come from it. I had my first outing as an entrepreneur in a meeting with the team at PMCH and they loved them and the story behind how they came to be. I remember hanging on to the power of the story behind the books. Our story is powerful.

I saw an ad in a paper from a local business who published books and I had a meeting at a coffee shop with the guy whose price was huge ($10,000) to publish one book. He did give me one piece of advice though, which I also held onto, and that was not to publish without a distribution network. This advice was way over my head at the time, but I took it on board. I knew there was another way for me, so I just kept doing what I was doing and continued evolving. I started writing for a website and in no time was asked to become their organic writer. I caught another bug - I wrote article after article - so many that the person who owned the website gave me the backend log in to upload my own articles because they were coming in too fast.

Then one day, it happened. I had an epiphany about why I had experienced a miscarriage. I felt an overwhelming urge to share my understanding with other women; other women who like me, were just expected to brush off their miscarriage and move on. Then NaNoWriMo appeared and even though it was only two days before I would have to commit to writing 1667 words a day for thirty days, I knew I had to try. I put together a possible outline and had a character (The Visitor) inspired by the epiphany. In November 2010 I wrote the heart centered novel that changed the course of my life. When it was finished, I set an intention of getting published, but did not have a clue where to begin, however one of the most valuable things I have learned about life and business is that it is our job in the law of attraction to request our desires; it is not our job to control how that comes to be. Never in my wildest dreams would I have ever foreseen the journey I was about to embark on.

Some background
In 2007, I was in Ireland and had lost a twin pregnancy. It was a traumatic experience for me as I had been through a dark time for a year and a half, previous to the loss and this was a glimmer of hope. I already had two boys and wasn't trying, but when I found out I was expecting, I wanted those babies more than anything in the world, so when I started bleeding, and after two weeks of trying to save them, losing them opened floodgates and I cried

rivers of tears for those babies and for the year and a half of lost magic moments that came before. Three years later, I found myself in Australia, having had two more healthy girls. My fourth child was four weeks old when I had the epiphany of the spiritual reason I experienced the loss, and as I am a great believer in 'when time and circumstance align, magic happens'.

I embraced all of the signs that led me to write a fictional novel in thirty days.

The Visitor was born, and after another series of circumstantial scenarios, I ended up publishing with an American press. It wasn't a passive experience and when I held that book in my hands, it really wasn't worth it. I had since written another book, and someone posed the question to me, 'Do you think you could help me publish my book?' This question gifted me a huge realisation that yes, I had learned so much about how a book is produced and I could potentially do it myself if I delved a bit deeper. So, I researched the print and distribution company that circulated my book and discovered that they had opened an office in Australia that very month (time and circumstance magic moment again!) I applied to become a publisher and was accepted. It was from that moment that I began sharing stories. The first anthology I produced was called Journey to Inner Light (it is being re-released late 2018). This book is filled with powerful stories from women who had endured tough times but have come through them sharing the best of themselves with the world.

That was the beginning and armed with passion, but not a lot of cash flow, I moved forward step by step towards the highest potential. I had no idea what that would end up being, so I left it open, allowing myself to be guided each step of the way. When I needed cash flow for the business, I thought of an idea that would generate income and ran with it. That helped me reach another stage and I did this for a few years until I began gaining some momentum.

My businesses

My businesses consist of many, all of which come under the umbrella of my Karen McDermott brand and all of which I am very passionate about. Each started with a seedling of an idea that was lovingly nurtured to fruition. My first business is a publishing company called Serenity Press, my second is the Making Magic Happen Academy (self-publishing imprint), Everything Publishing Academy (publishing academy), my author brand, Karen Weaver, Rose Weaver Books (children's books) and alongside that I am building three more businesses, Enrich Magazine - because everyone has a story to share, The Agency - an author/speaker collective, and a heart-centred UK-based endeavour called Weaver Birds Inc. See, I told you I am a serial entrepreneur! This is only possible because of the amazing people surrounding me.

The business I am most known for is Serenity Press. It has grown into a traditional publishing house, publishing fairytale collections by well-known authors. We host annual retreats and are finding our niche is in the fairytale genre. I am so proud that I have honoured the journey Serenity Press has had.

If I had not of allowed it to organically grow, it would not be the business it is today.

As my passion for publishing stemmed from my '**why**' of helping authors get published by educating them about the process of publishing, and how being an author is like owning a small business, I branched out to open my own self-publishing branch called the Making Magic Happen

Academy. From there, I launched my Everything Publishing Academy because I wanted to help as many people as possible to get published, so I created something that I wish I'd had when I began publishing. I have helped many publishing presses start, White Light Publishing House was the first publishing house that grew from my guidance in the initial stages, then Joanne Fedler Media, Monkey Blue Press, Gumnut Press, Rose Weaver Books and of course, Serenity Press. There quite possibly may be more by the time you read this story, and all because of my passion to help stories come to be and passions to reach their true potential. I am a great believer that everyone has a story to share, and I have made it my mission to help stories that may not have ever been told, get published.

How long have I been an entrepreneur?
I have been an entrepreneur for six years now. I wouldn't change it for the world as it allows me the freedom I need in life. I want to drop my kids to school in the morning and be there for them in the evenings. I want to be with them during the school holidays and if they are sick, I want to be the one to nurse them. This is often not achievable in a conventional job, so I had to create my own position.

I never realised that I would be embraced so warmly into the Australian business community and that my actions would inspire positive interactions from there. By pursuing my dreams, I also inspire others to be courageous to pursue their own potential. This makes my heart sing a melody of epic proportions. This is a very motivational source for me to access during the challenging days. My 'why' is strong and stems from a humanitarian side that drives me.

What kinds of challenges have you experienced with your business, and how did you overcome them?
I have had lots of challenges, but I seem to approach challenges with a growth mindset, which means that I don't see barriers, I see solutions, and I accept that it is all part of growing a business. My thinking on challenges is that they are there for us to learn from. I knew that if I wanted to create something amazing, I would have to get used to challenges as they are there to help us grow. My genius often resides in the eleventh hour. Even when I was studying for my humanities degree, I produced the best assignments the night before they were due to be handed in. I have identified that my strength is in focus, and I focus best when something has to be done, as it is then a priority for me. It is not ideal in some situations, but I will go above and beyond to make something happen. If you put in the effort, you will see the results.

What kind of support networks do you have? How do they help?
The first time I began networking was when my sixth child was born. I was awarded a scholarship to attend the AusMumpreneur conference. Wow, that conference blew my mind and made me come right out of my shell, instead of hiding behind a computer screen in my dining room. I realised that if I wanted to make an impact, I needed to raise my game and my profile and so with that in mind, I set a BFAG (Big Fat Audacious Goal) of hosting a retreat in an Irish Castle. It was a huge endeavour, but totally aligned with the passion I had for going home to see my family. It raised my profile so much and I won the AusMumpreneur award in 2016. I have been raising my game ever since. This year I have set a mission to be instrumental in the production of 100 books and here I am in April and have already reached 65 books. I feel very blessed that I have the support I have in all of the

endeavours I pursue. I don't do things alone anymore. In Serenity Press, I have the most wonderful partner Monique Mulligan, who keeps the ship afloat and makes our books the best they can possibly be. In my Karen McDermott brand, I have an amazing executive assistant called Veronica Gallipo. The editorial team around me is world class, and the designers and illustrators on my books are top class. This was a progressional process, and I was fortunate to attract high quality professionals who are aligned with my values.

What do you have planned for the future? What's coming up for you?
I have had huge amounts of success in everything I have pursued. Now it is time to navigate my focus towards the next ten years and beyond, so I have hired a mentor called Shevonne Joyce who is going to bring me to the next level and make me a global name. As this is my Do-Less-Be-More year, I am focusing primarily on my publishing academy and my books moving forward and inspiring people through my magazine, and I do believe a YouTube channel is on the cards in the not-so-distant future. I will continue to enjoy the journey all the more relaxed because I have reached a level of success that I am happy with and will grow so that I have a good foundation for my children to begin their journey from. I also now have deadlines to write for my Enlightenment Series, which is so exciting. My book, 'Everything Publishing' is being released in September 2018.

What words of wisdom do you have to share with other Mums who are thinking of starting their own business?
You don't have to know it all at the beginning. If you did, then the journey wouldn't be as interesting. Be open to opportunities coming from avenues that you would not

have even considered; often those opportunities will propel your business to new heights. So, when you start your business, yes have a business plan, but keep yourself open to it growing into something much bigger than you could have ever dreamt of initially. And yes, you can do it all whilst being the best mum you can be, too.

Karen

Christie Lyons

White Light Publishing House

I never really intended on running my own business. Five years ago, I was pregnant with my second child and was happy in my position as director of a community based childcare centre. I had worked in early childhood for over seven years and loved my job — so much so, that I had every intention of only taking a few months off, so I could return to work as soon as I could.

That was until my baby decided to come into the world almost six weeks early with a near-fatal heart condition. My little heart warrior Nate underwent open heart surgery when he was just ten days old to repair two holes in his tiny heart, and not only was this of course, a terrifying experience, it also had me reassessing every aspect of my life. Instead of being excited to return to my incredible career not long after his arrival, I was dreading it; wanting to focus all my energy on just being a Mum.

I had been running a small spiritual-based Facebook community with my sister in law, providing psychic readings and healings during my pregnancy, and had also been spending many an evening writing, after this passion of mine was reignited after contributing my own personal story in a book called, 'Journey to Inner Light'. I had no idea at that point that my entire working life was about to change in such a big way, but I did know that things were shifting — in every area of my life — and couldn't possibly imagine going back to practically *living* at work any longer.

Don't get me wrong — I actually enjoyed my job and looked forward to going to work every day. After all, I was working with children and families, and an incredible team of supportive staff. I was earning decent money (as decent as it can probably get for the industry) and knew I was good at my job. However, I was spending way too much of my time at work, and when I wasn't physically at work, I was taking work home with me. I knew this had to stop, and I agonized about what to do almost every day of my maternity leave. The closer it got to my return to work date, the more I stressed. We were paying off a mortgage, had a newborn baby and ten-year-old to care for, and my income was certainly going to be missed if I were to decide to leave. I played out different scenarios in my head — going back to work part-time, extending my maternity leave, and so forth — but none of them sat right with me.

I knew in my soul that I had to make an all-or-nothing choice. I would either return to work as promised, or I would resign.

Even though I knew this would mean some serious life changes for all of my family, I couldn't ignore my intuition any longer, so about a month before I was due to return to work, I sent in my resignation. Needless to say, everyone was shocked, and my staff were devastated with the news. What I felt though, was an instant weight lifted off my shoulders. Of course, I was scared about what was going to happen next, but I knew in my heart that it was the right decision. I do miss working with children even now, however four years on, I don't regret my decision for a second. The universe was pushing me in a brand-new direction and there was no way I could have ignored it.

Shortly after this decision was made, my eldest son came up with the idea to create a picture book about Nate's journey through his heart surgery – to help other families going through similar circumstances. I contacted my dear friend, Karen, who had not long been operating her own publishing house – then known as Inner Light Publishing (now Serenity Press). Being the beautiful soul that she is, she offered to donate her publishing services so that we could make the book a reality, and as soon as I saw the book in print, I just knew that I wanted to create more! Soon enough, I was coming up with idea after idea – asking Karen for quotes and advice left, right and centre, and I guess you could say, my creativity was sparked in a big way. I simply loved the feeling of holding my very own book in my hands, and seeing my words come to life on the pages is an experience that can't accurately be described until you feel it for yourself.

Karen must have sensed that something had been awakened in me, and she asked if we could make a time to have a chat. What I thought was going to be a conversation about all the ideas I'd had recently, turned into a business proposal and the excitement I felt from the moment Karen spoke about it was something I certainly wasn't expecting. Karen very generously offered to help me start my very *own* publishing house and boy oh boy, even though it was something I had never even contemplated, in my heart and soul, I knew it was meant to be. After all, when I was little, I had promised all my teachers that I would one day be an author and had even told my Mum that I was going to be a 'book maker'. Apparently, this was always going to happen, and the little girl inside of me reminded me of this fact (with help from Karen, of course).

With excitement, I told my sister in law (and business partner) about the concept and while she'd said it wasn't really 'her thing', she was all for including publishing and book sales in addition to the spiritual services we were already offering. With the creation of our very first books – which were children's books – White Light Publishing House was born in March 2014, and it wasn't very long before we signed up our very first client who had written a twelve-book astrology series. What a way to begin!

So, in between caring for a now almost six-month old baby, providing psychic and mediumship readings for clients, and teaching a tarot course, we gradually worked on editing and formatting our very first book series – all the while still learning how the publishing world works, and (sort of) knowing how to run a business of our own. It was all a bit of a whirlwind, and before I knew it, Nate's first birthday was approaching. This occasion was always going to be a special one, but considering all he'd been through, it was extra magical because we were so very blessed to have such a strong little boy in our lives. To add to the magic, it was at this time that I found out I was pregnant again!

It seems that the universe knew more about why I was meant to be a stay at home Mum than I did.

I knew from the moment I found out I was pregnant that this little bubba was going to be a girl. I had miscarried not long before I fell pregnant with Nate, and I had always sensed that this little girl was waiting to come into the world until after her big brother was born. And in May 2015, little Gracie entered the world. Unlike my experience with my two sons' births, Grace was born at almost full-term and I was able to have her in the ward with me right from the word 'go'. It was an entirely new experience for me, and every single day from the moment she came into the world, she has taught me something new – mostly reminding me of who I really am, and aspects of my inner child that need to resurface in my own life. What a blessing my daughter is.

In February 2016, my Mum and I decided to go on a trip together to Nepal. The moment we stepped off the plane, we could feel the magnificent energy and just knew it was going to be a life-changing experience. As well as connecting with some beautiful souls during our time over there, we returned home with a whole new perspective on life. The Nepalese people are such peaceful and kind souls, and while I already felt blessed for the life I have, being amongst such a refreshingly simple culture for two weeks had me filled with even more gratitude and love for my life.

I didn't know it at the time, but that trip proved to be the catalyst for some massive changes to the business. As Mum and I sat at the airport in Nepal waiting for our first flight home, I received a message from my business partner letting me know that once I returned home, she was walking away from the business. I was due home on the Saturday, and she would have nothing more to do with our business from Monday onwards. I was shocked, but somewhat not surprised at the same time. It was a little difficult to process the whole thing while in another country, however the moment I'd received that news, I began planning in my head, and did so all the way home. Rather than dwell on the extra workload I would now have or the fact that she'd made the decision to leave so abruptly, I felt it was better to focus on the positives – such as my newfound ability to run the business exactly the way I envisioned.

I set about making changes fairly quickly. I changed the name of the spiritual services business to align with my publishing house, removed what I felt was unnecessary, and introduced a more personal touch on social media and with clients in general. It was an interesting and exciting time in the first months after becoming the sole owner of the business. The only way I can describe it accurately is that the whole energy of the business seemed to shift dramatically once my business partner walked away. New publishing clients were suddenly drawn to me, my social media following doubled, and I even won Bronze as the AusMumpreneur Influencer of the Year award. What used to be a small, hobby-like business was suddenly becoming something that I couldn't keep up with on my own. I was loving how much the business was expanding, but at the same time, there were only so many hours in a day. My beautiful Mum, Lauren would spend tireless nights after work each day helping me as much as she possibly could, but we still couldn't keep up with the workload. It was in September 2016 that my dear Mum made her very own life-changing decision – much like I had two years earlier – to resign from her full-time corporate career to work alongside me.

To know that my mother has so much faith in me and the work I do is quite overwhelming – even now.

Clearly, the relationship I have with my Mum is pretty damn special. We spend almost every single day of the week working together, attend conferences and go on business trips together, and of course, that's in addition to usual family occasions. I am lucky in the fact that we have a 'no bullshit' kind of relationship. We are completely transparent with one another and keep each other grounded. We also share the same sense of humour, which helps in times when we are really under pressure or dealing with some kind of drama. Overall, we share the same values and agree on the direction we see White Light heading, and so my Mum not only 'works with me', but is now my business partner, which I am so very excited about.

It has now been just over two years since White Light changed direction, and while there have certainly been challenges along the way, the triumphs and rewards have far outweighed any hurdles we've been presented with. Even through the most frustrating times, we always, always see these challenges as a blessing in disguise, and take it on board as yet another lesson for us to learn. Most of the time when we are presented with what seems like a challenge at the time, it is purely a bit of a nudge to 'sort our shit out' before it really becomes a much bigger issue in the future. That's the way we like to think about it, anyway, and if it weren't for the odd 'kick up the bum' every now and then, we wouldn't be where we are today, which is a beautiful place indeed.

This time two years ago, White Light had one author (other than myself) and had released a total of three titles. We now have over thirty authors and have published more than forty titles (which include books, eBooks and oracle cards). The White Light family is growing every day - with new writers and artists coming on board to share their amazing gifts with the world, and the addition of new team members to help us expand even further. The vision that Mum and I have for the business is very exciting indeed, and with the development of our very own charity (in addition to many other projects) sometime in the not so distant future, we just know that this is only just the beginning for White Light.

I'll be the first to admit that running your own business is scary as shit at the best of times, and I've had to take a lot of risks, as well as continually step out of my comfort zone. But in doing so, the business has grown and more importantly, I have grown. If I am ever questioning any aspect of my business, or need to make a decision, my answer can always be found quite easily when I go back to my 'why'; reminding myself of what I am truly passionate about, and the reason I started this business in the first place.

Figure out who you are separate from your family, and the man or woman you're in a relationship with. Find who you are in this world and what you need to feel good alone. I think that's the most important thing in life. Find a sense of self because with that, you can do anything else.

-Angelina Jolie

More about our authors

Ali Knights

KIN balance

Ali Knights is a mother of two and founder of KIN balance. Launched in 2015, KIN balance is a natural therapy that helps people reduce overwhelm and anxiety and connect to who they truly are by balancing their body, mind and spirit.

Living in rural South Australia, Ali's aim is to make the alternative mainstream and accessible to all. She supports families and individuals of all ages, from newborn babies to the elderly all over Australia.

A teacher by trade, she also has a passion for supporting the mental health of teenagers and through this has had two onsite school clinics in regional SA.

Website: www.kinbalance.com.au

Social Media: www.facebook.com/kinbalance

Ashley Brown

Sosocii Pty Ltd

Ashley is based in the beautiful Yarra Ranges of Victoria and busily raising three children, aged five years and under. She is a former primary school teacher who sought a career change following the birth of her eldest daughter. Ashley has been a Virtual Assistant for over three years, and her main areas of focus include: social media management, Facebook ad campaigns, Google Ad Words, email marketing, press releases, ghost writing blogs and drafting copy for websites and apps. She still feels very inspired by the ever-evolving nature of the business sector and enjoys the variety of industries she has been lucky enough to work with. Ashley gets a massive thrill out of engaging with other business owners when she facilitates various local networking events. She loves that women can work together to support each other's ambitions and has a particular passion for working with other mums in business.

Website: www.sosocii.com

Social Media: www.facebook.com/sosociisolutions

Bronte Spicer

Soul Worker Academy

Bronte Spicer is a mother of two, Principal of the Soul Worker Academy and Teacher for spiritual, entrepreneurial Mums. As an Advanced Meditation Teacher, Intuitive Reader and Healer, Bronte specialises in helping women to courageously follow their path of sacred service.

Crippled with depression for over a decade of her life, Bronte experienced how self-doubt and self-worth stopped her from pursuing what her heart desired. For many years, she hid inside the spiritual closet, overwhelmed by her soul purpose and paralysed by fear. On her journey of unlocking her own soul potential, Bronte found the freedom and fulfillment to do the work her soul was always yearning to do. In just over twelve months, Bronte has led more than 30 women to be graduates of the Soul Worker Academy so they too, can bring their soul creations to the world, confidently showcase their work with their growing social media tribe and witness the wild transformations in their clients from their own creations.

Bronte holds a Bachelor of Education/Bachelor of Sport & Outdoor Recreation from Monash University and is a Reiki Practitioner. She facilitates classes, workshops and retreats, and regularly presents at public engagement events across Victoria, Australia. She has been interviewed by Australia's most comprehensive natural therapy magazine, Wellbeing Magazine and led the Marketing Team at the Australian Centre for Holistic Studies. Bronte is currently writing her own spiritual guidebook to help more women leap with faith, so they too can express who they truly are and pursue the light-filled work of their soul.

Website:
www.soulworkeracademy.co

Social Media:
www.facebook.com/soulworkeracademy

Ellen Lorraine Niemeier

Soul Level Healing LLC

Ellen Lorraine Niemeier has nurtured a deep interest in energy medicine, energy work, healing, psychic work and miracles for many years. She has worked in several industries in multiple capacities, including teaching very young children through adults, facilitating music therapy for children and adults, music performance, insurance and admin work, restaurant and more. After having her baby, she followed her heart, and learned how to read the Akashic Records, first in the modality of Soul Realignment®, then continued her studies through the World Metaphysical Association. She is a Certified Advanced Soul Realignment® Practitioner and Certified Akashic Records Master Reader. She serves clients worldwide in her business, Soul-Level Healing LLC. Ellen has a passion for serving individuals, children and parents to assist them to discover themselves, align to their Soul-Level divinity, gain deep insight into their relationships with one another, and offers support with energy work to create the life they really want.

Website: www.soullevelhealing.com

Social Media: www.facebook.com/soullevelhealing117

Hayley Scott

haylelyscott.com.au

Hayley is passionate about many things in life, but she feels truly at her best when she is working with people and assisting in their development. She gets real satisfaction when she is able to facilitate learning and growth opportunities for individuals. Hayley is fascinated by human behaviour and continues to develop her knowledge in the area of peak performance and what it takes for people flourish. Stand still long enough and she will share with you her latest learning's on topics including: emotional intelligence, mindfulness, neuroscience, leadership, positive psychology and so much more!

Hayley's experience spans over fifteen years in various leadership roles and more recently as a HR professional. Hayley's latest venture sees her offering coaching services and, as a lover of the stage, she also performs the role of Master of Ceremonies (MC) at conferences, networking events and charity functions. Hayley enjoys writing and finally decided to hit 'publish' on her first blog post with the intention of writing more frequently.

Hailing from the U.K., Hayley settled in Western Australia fifteen years ago, loving all that Australia has to offer. She sometimes talks a lot (ok, make that: she often talks a lot), she is not terribly organised and at times wears many different hats to survive another crazy week. During the winter months Hayley loves to don her running gear and hit the pavement as often as possible for a run. And during summer, you will find her by the pool with a book in one hand and a glass of something sparkling in the other.

Website: www.hayleyscott.com.au

Social Media:
www.instagram/hayley_scott

Jennifer Forest

Carrot Patch Content

Jennifer Forest is an interpretative curator and writer with a focus on telling the stories of Australia's land and people, past and present.

Website: www.carrotpatch.com.au

Joanne Giles

BROWSE

Joanne Giles is the founder at BROWSE Events in Sydney, Australia, where she inspires businesses and individuals alike to grow through the events she creates. She grew up in South Africa and then the UK before emigrating to Australia. Before fulfilling her dream of running her own business, she gained valuable life experience working in a vast array of industries from Nuclear Power to Her Majesty's Prison Service. She lives by the beach on the Central Coast of NSW with her husband, two children and golden retriever.

Website: www.browseau.com

Social Media: www.facebook.com/browseau

Kelly McDonald

Garden Babies Fairy Art

Storyteller, magician, lover of faerie tales and magic, Kelly is inspired by tales of old in both her artwork, which can be found at www.gardenbabiesfairyart.com and writing.

Owning, operating and working in childcare centres and kinders since she was 16 years old, Kelly has been storytelling as the magical faerie Crystall for the past 25 years. She can still be found fluttering her wings and performing on occasion.

Magic, faerie law, paranormal activity and historical stories including those three elements

Website: www.gardenbabiesfairyart.com

Social Media: www.facebook.com/gardenbabiesfairyart

Natalee Anderson

Fat Burning Women

Natalee Anderson is a Nutritional Therapist, Personal Trainer, Life Coach and Healer who has supported hundreds of women to heal their body and soul through hormone balance, nutritional medicine, metabolic resets, stored emotional release, positive psychology, essential oils, and lifestyle strategies. Founder of Fat Burning Women, writer and speaker, Natalee eloquently makes health simple by discovering people's blind spots, stripping back all the layers dulling their shine and providing the roadmap back home to the true self.

Website: www.fatburningwomen.com

Social Media: www.facebook.com/Fatburningwomen

Rochelle Muscat

Pop the Balloon! Children's Parties & Events

Rochelle is the owner and creative mind behind Pop the Balloon! Children's Parties & Events – a fun and vibrant children's party styling and entertainment business. Rochelle also owns and operates Party Utopia Events – where she offers a tailored and personalised event styling service for her clients who are desiring something that is unique and truly memorable for their special celebration.

Based on the picturesque NSW Central Coast, Rochelle is a NSW Justice of the Peace and a married mother of 3 beautiful children who inspire her every day to laugh, dream bigger and live in the moment (and to put extra lollies in the party bags!). Always looking at life from a different perspective, Rochelle seeks to inspire others to be their best self, shake off that which is holding them back, and to not be bothered by the negative opinions of others. At the end of the day, life is about what makes your heart sing and your soul soar – a sentiment that shines through in every party she creates and celebrates with her clients.

Website:
www.poptheballoonchildrenspartiesandevents.com.au

Social Media:
www.facebook.com/PopTheBalloonChildrensPartiesAndEvents

Samantha Young

Samantha brings a unique combination of senior management and commercial experience, psychological intervention skills and Masters-level formal education in both business and psychology to her clinical, training, coaching and consulting work. She has led large teams, advised CEOs and Boards on strategic issues and routinely provides consulting advice to private and public sector organisations on complex human resource matters, training and development, enhancing employee engagement and wellbeing and operational matters.

Samantha has worked as a Consultant with Boston Consulting Group, Sales & Marketing Manager for The Body Shop and Strategy Manager for Myer Grace Bros. Samantha holds Bachelor and Postgraduate qualifications in business and psychology, including a master's Degree in clinical psychology and an MBA from Melbourne University. Samantha has completed the Company Director's Course and is a member of the Australian Psychological Society.

Samantha is passionate about helping people to think, feel and perform better at individual, team and organisational levels. She is Managing Director for Human Psychology, one of Adelaide's largest psychological services providers with a team of 15 people. Samantha is a single Mum to two girls and two dogs and is still trying to perfect the art of work: life integration as a life goal!

Website: www.humanpsychology.com.au

Social Media: www.facebook.com/humanpsychology.com.au

Susanna Heiskanen

Tuutu

Susanna Heiskanen is the co-founder and CEO of Tuutu. Tuutu sell a baby box that is a cardboard box with sustainable baby essentials for parents to be. The box double as a bed with mattress that comes with the box. These clever boxes have been around in Finland for decades where the government gives one for the parents for free of charge. Sustainability is important on all the products that Tuutu uses. All the products are selected due their sustainability, multifunction or recycle nature.

Website: www.tuutu.com.au

Social Media: www.facebook.com/TuutuBabyBox

Talita Sheedy

Lahlita Natural Medicine

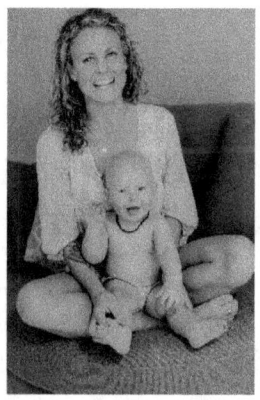

Talita lives mindfully on the Sunshine Coast, Queensland with her Husband and two children. She grew up on a small hobby farm inland but due to her love for the beach, once old enough she moved to be beside the ocean. Talita is ignited by all things natural, holistic and living a conscious lifestyle, from food to yoga. She says that she is lucky to have a career that she loves and is specifically passionate about pregnancy, fertility and children's health.

Website: www.lahlita.com.au

Social Media: www.facebook.com/lahlitanaturalmedicine

Tracey Farrelly

Angels n Beyond

Internationally renowned Psychic Medium, Tracey Farrelly, has worked on Psychic TV, Mind Body Spirit Festivals, Platform work and Corporate Events. Tracey is also a Certified Reiki Practitioner (Certified in Reiki I & Reiki II), and a published author.

Tracey is a compassionate and confidential person you can feel safe to come to for a private reading. Loved ones in spirit around a client may bring through information (past, present and future) OR come to visit and give confirmation to the client to let them know they are still around them. A simple way of describing what Tracey sees is that she sees images as if on a TV screen and spirit guides tell Tracey information that she then passes onto the client.

Angels n Beyond
CONVERSATIONS WITH SPIRIT

Website: www.angelsnbeyond.com.au

Ruchika Rawat

Roo and Joey

Ruchika Rawat is the Founder of Roo and Joey. She has an impressive background in community engagement and preventive and health promotion project planning, implementation and monitoring before becoming an entrepreneur. She is actively involved in strategic business development and market planning; supporting women in business from multicultural backgrounds. She is the driver of Roo and Joey's mission of blossoming Mums and Bubs! She manages the day to day operations of the organisation, its community and strategy and guides the business culture of the collective as an inclusive, supportive and innovative group.

She strongly advocates the cause of gender equality and financial freedom for females and is actively involved in promotion and awareness as a member of the United Nations Women National Committee, Australia. She also gives back by supporting education of underprivileged children in the developing world. She strongly feels for environment sustainability and promotes it on various platforms.

Ruchika has landed coverage in various outlets in Australia and Asia including The Muse, Indus Age and Australian Indian community newspapers and magazines like Indian Sun, Indian Voice and The Indian Telegraph.

Website: www.rooandjoey.com.au

Social Media: www.facebook.com/rooandjoey

Laura McNally

Monkey Blue Press

Laura Quinn is a new and upcoming Children's book Creator and Author. After receiving a place in the Making Magic happen Academy, Laura created her own brand of children's books that became an overnight success.

Laura's first book, 'Monkey Blue and Friends' came from her first collection and after visiting with her illustrator she was inspired to write some Halloween stories. 'What on Earth' then became her second collection. She is currently living back on her home turf in Ireland and is adding to her first two collections, as well as releasing a third collection later in 2018.

Laura always had a passion for writing and was told she had a flair for it. After getting back on her feet after having her first baby, she knew she had an itch and regardless of her beautiful son, she knew she wouldn't feel fulfilled until she got that itch and gave it an almighty scratch, which she did.

Laura has been approached to work alongside some amazing illustrators and is now beginning her first co-write, 'My Mum's Not Different'.

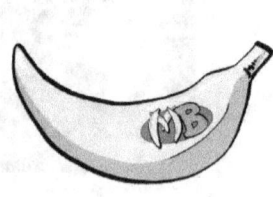

Website: www.monkeybluepress.com

Anu Sawhney

Bidiliia

Anuradha 'Anu' Sawhney is a passionate entrepreneur who leads from her heart. She has worked for several high-profile fashion designers across the globe and more closely, here in Australia. After having her daughter, her pre-existing R.A combined with hormonal changes lead her into going through multiple joint replacements. It is in hospitals and rehabilitation that she re-ignited her passion for design and connecting with artisans to create her jewelry brand, Bidiliia.

At Bidiliia, she combines exceptional design and craftsmanship, with honourable ethics and a need for ethical and sustainable fashion jewelry and ensures affordability to bridge the gap. She designs for all women and creates jewelry that makes women look amazing. Anu has created a more sustainable and fairer work environment for craftsmen. Her skill at design and her unending passion to do good and lead from the heart is honourable and admirable.

Website: www.bidiliia.com

Social Media: www.facebook.com/bidiliia

Claire Orange

BEST Programs 4 Kids

Firstly, and most importantly, Claire is the mum of four boys. She is also a therapist, author, media spokesperson, speaker and advocate for better outcomes for children everywhere. As the co-director of BEST Programs 4 Kids, Claire has co-authored a whole-of-school social and emotional wellbeing curriculum that is used in hundreds of schools across Australia and internationally, too. With twenty-five years of experience in health and education, Claire is passionate about every child, parent and school community being empowered, educated and engaged in the journey towards glowing mental health, resilience and a lifetime of flourishing.

Website: www.bestprograms4kids.com

Social Media: www.facebook.com/BESTPrograms4Kids

Emma Lovell

CoziGo – Sleep on the Go

Emma Lovell. Wife. Mother. Entrepreneur. Innovator. Change-Maker. Creator.

Emma Lovell is originally from the UK. She resides in Manly, Sydney with her supportive husband and two children.

Emma's light bulb moment was the outcome of flying and using an inflight bassinet with a very distracted and overtired baby. She used masking tape and a sheet to try and create an inflight canopy for her baby. Emma also grew frustrated when the blanket covering her daughter's pram would fly off, fall off or get pulled off. CoziGo is the solution to trying to get a tired baby to sleep on a plane or when out and about with one's pram.

Emma appeared on Shark Tank and courageously won over investor Janine Allis from Boost Juice.

Emma's favourite quote is: "The harder I work, the luckier I get." Thomas Jefferson

Website: www.cozigo.com

Social Media: www.facebook.com/cozigo

Jessica McCarroll

First in Breast Dressed

I am a Mum first, a wife, a physio and a friend. My journey to be a Mumpreneur started during the fourth trimester with my first boy. My business is built on a longing to help others as well as beginning to heal myself.

Website: www.firstinbreastdressed.com

Social Media: www.facebook.com/firstinbreastdressed

Karen Koutsodontis

The Travelling Kitchen

Travelling Kitchen founder Karen Koutsodontis is a food technology teacher, mother of three and visionary leader who first saw that the gap between primary school eating habits and secondary school needs closing.

The Travelling Kitchen visits primary schools, kindergartens, after-school care programs, Children's festivals and school holiday programs to help inspire and educate children about healthy eating and the skills to enjoy and make healthy food.

Website: www.thetravellingkitchen.com.au

Social Media:
www.facebook.com/thetravellingkitchenincursions

Katharine Rattray

Kat & Fox

If there were a meaning in the dictionary for 'Katharine Rattray' it would be 'wonderous creative ball of vibrant energy'.

Katharine is a pommy ex pat mother of three and resides in country Victoria, Australia. She has always worked in the creative arts. Preliminary she trained in Fine Arts and then onto university to study Interior Design. This led her to travel the world, finally residing and becoming a citizen of Australia.

Over a twelve-year period, Katharine has juggled motherhood, working in her own small side businesses and teaching her skills to others at a local TAFE. She began by running her own interior design business 'Pommigranite Rooms by design'. This transformed into 'Doodlebugs': hand drawn greeting cards and commissioned artworks for children. Finally, she changed the name and created the award-winning brand 'Kat & Fox'. Here she found a way to apply her quirky illustrations onto bed linen, wall art and even illustrated her own children's book 'Bird Boy & Wren'.

From Fine Artist, to Interior Designer, to Creative Arts teacher, to Illustrator and Textile Designer, her skills have evolved with her creative passions shining through. Katharine's business ventures were always only small sidelines and now have eventuated into her only career focus in the form of 'Kat & Fox'. Here she stands tall, happy and true to herself.

Website: www.katandfox.com.au

Social Media: www.facebook.com/katandfox

Melissa Woodward

Evolution Health Services

Melissa is a Mum, Wife, Remedial Massage Therapist and Women's Health Coach in her business, Evolution Health Services. Melissa is passionate about working with women through all stages of pregnancy and into motherhood. She provides Remedial Massage during pregnancy and is experienced in assisting women return to exercise post baby. Melissa understands the struggles to fall pregnant, what happens to the body during pregnancy and how to safely recover after a c-section as well as abdominal separation.

Melissa spends her days with clients in the clinic, outdoors in fitness classes with mums, networking with her favourite local business owners and writing content to share with her clients. Her health philosophy is focused on helping clients make small regular changes to their lifestyle, inclusiveness regardless of size or shape and body positivity. She believes in educating to empower clients to make the best decisions for their personal health and circumstances.

Website:
www.evolutionhealthservices.com.au

Social Media:
www.facebook.com/evolutionhealthservices

Karen McDermott

Serenity Press

Karen Mc Dermott, founder of Serenity Press, Making Magic Happen Academy and Everything Publishing Academy is an award-winning entrepreneur, multi-genre author of over twenty books, mentor and renowned speaker. She's also an advanced Law of Attraction practitioner who teaches people how to attract anything they want into their lives. Her annual retreats are sought after events with featured famous guests.

Her motto is: Where there is a will, there is always a way.

Her quote is: When time and circumstance align, magic happens.

Karen is passionate about sharing her extensive knowledge and vibrant energy with others. She has a 'no excuse' policy, if she can do it, anyone can.

Website:
www.karenmcdermott.com.au

Social Media:
www.facebook.com/serenitypresspublishing

KAREN MCDERMOTT
Publisher & Public Speaker

Christie Lyons

White Light Publishing House

Founder of White Light Publishing House, Christie is a mother of a teenager and two young children. Previously a childcare centre director, she has several years' experience and holds qualifications in early childhood education and is passionate about children's rights and emotional well-being.

Her love of writing was reignited after she miscarried back in 2012 and with the encouragement of her now dear friend Karen McDermott, her very own publishing house was born.

As well as helping writers around the world's dreams come true, Christie is also a psychic medium and healer, and hopes to one day open her very own bricks and mortar book shop/writer's café.

Website: www.whitelightpublishing.com.au

Social Media: www.facebook.com/whitelightpublishing

Next time, ask: what's the worst that will happen? Then push yourself a little further than you dare. Once you start to speak, people will yell at you. They will interrupt you, put you down and suggest it's personal. And the world won't end ... And the speaking will get easier and easier. And you will find you have fallen in love with your own vision, which you may never have realized you had. And you will lose some friends and lovers and realize you don't miss them. And new ones will find you and cherish you ... And at last you'll know with surpassing certainty that only one thing is more frightening than speaking your truth. And that is not speaking.

– **Audre Lorde**

See more of our titles at:
www.whitelightshop.com

www.ingramcontent.com/pod-product-compliance
Lightning Source LLC
Chambersburg PA
CBHW071855290426
44110CB00013B/1149